Christopher Chikwanah

EMBRACING CHANGE

Reflections from a life story

Acknowledgements

Special thanks and gratitude to my wife, Yvonne, who, as always, has supported me unfailingly in my pursuits and endeavours.

In memory of my mother, the late Cecilia Tambudzai Chikwanah, who invested her all into me to give me the life I have today. A true heroine, and a true role model who defied all the odds for my success.

To my children, Christopher Jnr and Tiffany: I hope I have been the father to you that I never had, and I trust that I have modelled before you a life worthy of emulating.

My big sisters, Veronica and Jean … love you guys!

Appreciation to Bishop Gerri Di Somma, my pastor and mentor, for teaching me the principles of God's kingdom and inspiring me to pursue manhood that is synonymous with Christlikeness!

Misheck Saineti for directing me and encouraging me to be anchored in the faith.

Contents

Foreword

When I was asked to write a foreword for Christopher's book, *Embracing Change*, little did I expect it to be a mini self-help book based on a journey very similar to my own, with great principles of truth and nuggets of wisdom attached to it.

While reading, a scripture from the book of Revelation sprang to mind. It's found in chapter 12 verse 11: *"And they overcame him because of the blood of the Lamb and because of the word of their testimony, and they did not love their life even when faced with death."*

This scripture and this book describe Christopher's journey of faith; it is not Christopher's full testimony, but it is one that depicts a journey fraught with pain, frustration and disappointment that, with God's help, the truth of God's Word and the leading of the Holy Spirit turned into a triumphal declaration of God's salvation.

Christopher overcame cultural challenges, social changes and emotional upheaval with the application of time-tested principles and patterns in the Bible, which can only lead to promotion, peace and prosperity.

I would encourage the reader to carefully note the processes shared and, if facing a crisis of circumstances and change, to apply the steps to overcome as Christopher so clearly demonstrates in this book.

I was tempted to edit some of the colloquial expressions in the book to make it more readable to audiences not familiar with them. However, I realised that by doing so, it would have completely taken away from the Christopher I know. I could almost hear him speaking while I was reading, and I loved that!

Christopher has a great testimony. His love for God is undeniable, the love he lavishes on his wife is evident, and it is a delight to be with his children. The Bible speaks of these as qualities of a mature man who has first learned to master himself before indulging in teaching others about life.

I trust that as you read this book, you will not just read to gain information but to receive revelation for your own journey through and towards change. Remember, change is here to stay, so learn how to embrace it.

Bishop Gerri Di Somma

Founder and Lead Minister of Carmel Ministries International, Carmel Global Ministries Inc and Carmel Bible College.

"The key to happiness is to be able to change pain into pleasure, darkness into light and sorrow into joy.
This can occur only if we have the courage to change."

(Unknown)

Introduction

"Therefore, since we have so great a cloud of witnesses surrounding us, let us also lay aside every encumbrance and the sin which so easily entangles us, and let us run with endurance the race that is set before us, fixing our eyes on Jesus, the author and perfecter of faith, who for the joy set before Him endured the cross, despising the shame, and has sat down at the right hand of the throne of God." (Hebrews 12:1-2).

The **EVENT** of **CHANGE** is something that has been around for a very long time. It has transcended generations and millennia and has been the source of many a debate. It is a subject about which many books have been written, and a multitude of opinions have been voiced and expressed. Change is something that cannot be avoided, yet some have embraced it, and others have not.

My purpose for writing this book is not to add to the plethora of arguments, views and opinions regarding change; instead, my aim is to approach and communicate the power of embracing change – not from an intellectual, theoretical or anecdotal perspective but from an experiential perspective.

I say this because I am a man who has faced and undertaken a lot of change processes – spiritually, geographically, professionally, relationally, socially and in other aspects of life – and I believe that I can inspire others to embrace their own journeys of change proactively and not reactively, on the front foot rather than the back foot.

> *"Change is the law of life.*
> *And those who look only to the past or present*
> *are certain to miss the future."*
>
> (John F. Kennedy)[1]

This book is very special to me in many respects, but especially in one: it has given me the courage and boldness to do what I would not normally do, and that is to lay bare my life. I am, by nature, a very private individual, as those who know me well would attest. I do not often share my life experiences, as I have tended to avoid the negative emotions some of those experiences evoke.

It is my hope that you, the reader, will be encouraged by the insights I have gleaned and learned on my journey through change. I trust that the principles and concepts shared therein will inspire, direct and bring a much different perspective when you are faced with change. Perhaps, they will even help you respond differently to change!

Let me state this at the outset: change is a **PROCESS**; it is very important for me to acknowledge that each individual's circumstances and experiences will vary, but I believe some parallels can be drawn nonetheless. As I reflected on the various changes that I have encountered, the letter **P** kept flashing in my mind, and I could not shake it off. Eventually, I realised that it represented patterns.

When I further analysed each process or phase of change I have been through, it became very clear that each was characterised by (or was usually typified by) certain **PATTERNS** and **PRINCIPLES**. These patterns and principles had been present whenever I encountered change, even when I was not consciously aware of them. These are the **Ps** of change that I will refer to throughout this book.

> *"Understanding of life begins with the understanding of patterns."*
>
> (Fritjof Capra)[2]

Even though these patterns are present in most people's journeys of change, one can easily fail to identify them and totally miss them – as was the case in my own life, so it can be in your life, too! It is important to know and identify these patterns because they will heavily influence and inform how we face, manage and handle change.

Change is always happening around us. In which case, why do people fail to recognise the patterns? I believe it's because change is not always in the spectacular or the dramatic. Think about it: with each ticking second, we are older by one second. In other words, we have entered a place in time, even by that short and seemingly insignificant small interval of time, that we have never been in before. That's change! And guess what? It happens 86,400 times every single day!

Ecclesiastes tells us in chapter 3 verses 1 and 2 that *"There is an appointed time for everything. And there is a time for every event under heaven – A time to..."* I like the part that says, *'A time to'* – you can put anything after that statement that is representative of your change! A time to go to nursery; a time to go to junior school; a time to go to university; a time to encounter the Lord; a time to be married; sadly, a time to die; and so forth.

> *"Timing is everything.*
> *If it's meant to happen, it will,*
> *at the right time for the right reasons."*
>
> (Unknown)

In the simplest terms possible, this illustrates that there will be change in various aspects of life and that change will come at its appointed time. Note that the appointed time of change may not always appear or occur at a time that is convenient or appropriate to you, but there *is* an appointed time!

In his hardest time, Job knew that change would come; he probably did not know the 'when, the why or the how', but he acknowledged the inevitability of change, saying, *"…all the days of my appointed time will I wait, till my **change** come."* (Job 14:14, KJV).

In spite of the changes we encounter, our heavenly Father knows what lies ahead, and He has His plans for us clearly laid out, even though we may not know them yet. The changes we face have not and will never catch Him by surprise. I cannot imagine God ever saying, "Oops, even I never saw that coming!" We, therefore, are the ones who need to be in tune with what God is doing and with what He has planned for us. He gives us guaranteed life *"plans for welfare and not for calamity to give you a future and a hope."* (Jeremiah 29:11).

Even though God does not change, He does initiate change for our good. To be absolutely clear, He changes situations rather than His nature – all one needs to do is to go to the beginning, to the book of Genesis. There was an undesirable status quo in place, and change was needed. Order needed to be established over chaos, light over darkness, fruitfulness over barrenness, life over death. God had to initiate change, and the outcome of that change was good (Genesis 1).

The New Testament writer, James, the brother of Jesus, echoes this truth in his letter to the early Christians: *"Every good thing given and every perfect gift is from above, coming down from the Father of lights, with whom there is no variation or shifting shadow."* (James 1:17).

God always sees the good in what He changes. Yet, as people created in the image of God, we struggle to see the good in the change(s) we face and encounter. I am not solely referring to the actual processes, because from my own experiences, not all the processes were pleasurable or good. And the problem is that we tend to become preoccupied with what we are experiencing and going through rather than focussing on the end results of the change. However, with the right mindset, we can press through the tough processes and be strengthened in and by them. The key is that our eyes must be on the good outcome.

Carrying a child in the womb for nine months must be a really uncomfortable change. Now some may say, "Christopher, you're a man … what do you know about the discomforts of pregnancy?" Well, when my wife was pregnant with our twins, she never had a single day of morning sickness – I was the one who experienced sickness in the mornings, so I know what I'm talking about!

The discomfort of pregnancy then continues to the labour pains and finally to the birth itself. During pregnancy, labour and birth, there is only one thing at the fore of every mother's mind … THE BABY! All of the discomfort and pain is soon forgotten when the end result (the baby, the good) comes. And some women even go on to have more than one child – how about that?!

Jesus Christ, our Lord, set this example when He lived a perfect and sinless life on earth. He knew the pain that awaited Him at His death; however, He did not focus on the pain, but the very good end result – the salvation and restoration of man, you and I!

In fact, the Bible does not even call it His pain, but His joy, as seen in verse 2 of Hebrews 12, which says: *"...looking unto Jesus, the author and finisher of our faith, who for the **joy** that was set before Him endured the cross, despising the shame, and has sat down at the right hand of the throne of God."* (NKJV).

The BIG question is this: how are you going to embrace the inevitable change that will come your way?

"Your life does not get better by chance, it gets better by change."

(Jim Rohn)[3]

"Everyone sees what you appear to be, few experience what you really are."

(Niccolò Machiavelli)[1]

Chapter One

The Man Behind the Story

The aim of this chapter is not to go too deeply into the history of my life, as that would probably entail writing an entirely separate book. I am merely going to outline the major aspects and points relevant to my journey of change.

I hope that you will gain some insights into where I have come from, and I trust that through the progression of the book, you will be able to see and appreciate what I have been through and where God has brought me. This is not to claim I have attained all; I am still a work in progress, striving to achieve, even by a small measure, what God has ordained for me.

I was born in Zambia, the youngest of three; I have two older sisters, and we were raised by my mother, who was a single parent. We grew up as a very close-knit family. As a child, I was oblivious of the challenges my mother faced because we seemed to have what we needed. Note that I used the word 'needed' and not 'wanted'. I did not get many of my 'wants', but I had my 'needs' met. And when I say 'needs', I'm talking about the basic essentials, things necessary for life – we did not have the 'wants' of toys, bicycles, a television or even a radio. We did have a vinyl record player, though! I remember some of the old songs my mother used to play (when music was proper music), and this may be something that has strongly influenced and ignited my passion for music!

What we lacked in material possessions was more than made up for in love (and discipline!). My mother had a very strong work ethic. As the only male child, and being the last born, one would have thought I would have been pampered and spoiled rotten … alas, no! Mother ensured that I was competent in the same life-skills that were imparted to the girls.

Household chores, such as cleaning, laundry, ironing, cooking and the like were the order of the day. At times, I would question if she was really my mother because she made me work so hard! But now, **I am ever so grateful** for her training and input that has equipped me to live life so well.

I firmly believe this is what has made me the capable man I am today, possessing the same work ethic as my dear mother. I am not one to shy away from what needs doing, and I am in a strong position to serve my family and those around me. I often wonder how many other people had a parent (or parents) like mine! I'm sure you can guess that I have taken the same approach as my mother with my own children! Truly, this great woman's vision and legacy live on in us!

> *"Legacy is not leaving something for people, but leaving something in people."*
>
> (Peter Strople)[2]

It was only as I advanced in age that I started to become more aware of the fact that my mother was facing a lot of challenges. That childhood oblivion faded as I became more conscious of the reality of her life. Sometimes, I would see her crying, presumably due to the hardships of raising three children on her own with limited resources, and she was unaware that I was watching her. We plodded along with life until, one day, Mum was involved in a car accident that left her with a very bad fracture in one of her arms. It meant that she could not work for a very long time.

We had a supportive family network of aunts and uncles, but at that time, Zambia was in a very bad economic state, and I can only presume it was difficult to live off people who themselves had their own needs to take care of.

It was at this time that I also started feeling the void of having no father, and I became somewhat embittered at not having 'my dad' around. I would say to myself, "If Dad were around, we would not be struggling like this, and things would be a lot better for us." I cannot say with certainty that things would have been better, but to my logic, that was the only conceivable outcome. In my mind, dads could sort out anything. And you know what? I don't think that was an unreasonable way of thinking!

Of course, we all have expectations, and at times those expectations are met, but sometimes they are not, and we will be disappointed. I had to live with some of the disappointments that life brought my way. What I wanted was the ideal scenario, but the truth is that, in life, not everything is ideal, so we have to live with the real.

> *"Life is a journey that must be travelled no matter how bad the roads and accommodations."*
>
> (Oliver Goldsmith)[3]

"Sometimes it's the journey that teaches you a lot about your destination."

(Drake)[1]

Chapter Two

The Journey Begins

At the age of 10, my family (my mother, one of my sisters and I) emigrated to Zimbabwe. My eldest sister was at a crucial level in her education where uprooting her would not have been to her benefit. I can only speculate that, at the time we emigrated, Zimbabwe had the promise of better economic and educational prospects.

Since I was a child, I did not have any choice or any say in the matter! We've already noted that change *will* come – there's a well-known saying that **the only constant in life is change**; at times, you'll have a say in it, and at other times, you won't! But it will come at some point or another!

The move to Zimbabwe heralded the beginning of my journey through several processes of change. Leaving Zambia meant I had to leave what I was **familiar** with – school, friends, my neighbourhood, cousins and so much more. Living in Zimbabwe dictated and necessitated learning a new language, forming new friends, adapting to a different system of education and culture, and so forth.

Life in Zimbabwe presented its own challenges. Could this be the proverbial, 'The grass is always greener on the other side'? Maybe not in all respects! Let us see how the journey unfolded.

More than anything, I missed my big sister, and it felt like the close-knit family unit I was so accustomed to had been fragmented. Mother was working, but her low income meant that, on most occasions, we had more month than we had money. It may be a hard thought for some, but imagine your electricity being cut off, barely making the rent, walking several miles to and from school every day as there was no bus fare; I'm sure some of you are getting a glimpse of the picture, and I will not belabour the point.

> *"Don't expect everyone to understand your journey, especially if they have never walked your path."*
>
> (Unknown)

I was in the latter half of primary school when we moved to Zimbabwe, and just as I was settling, I completed primary school and went to high school. Yet again, I had to leave what was familiar to me – this time, it was my 'primary school comfort zone' – and form new friendships and adapt to new dynamics. This change was very significant in that even my mentality and mindset had to adjust and transcend to a higher level of functioning and thinking.

I will briefly mention that my eldest sister had, by this time, joined us in Zimbabwe. With more mouths to feed and the need for a bigger place to live, came more financial pressures. However, my sisters, though still also in full-time education, managed to do some casual work here and there to contribute towards the family's needs.

I believe it was in high school that I grew up very quickly (though there are some people who did not know me very well who would disagree, and respectfully, that is their prerogative). I used to play rugby, and after my school matches, I would go and watch the provincial teams or the national team play. It was during one of those times that an opportunity to work arose (doing the scoreboard, selling match programs, etc.).

During a good weekend, I could make enough money to buy a week's worth of groceries. That kind of money in a youngster's hands could have meant sweets, ice cream and all sorts of frivolous indulgences! But it was not so with this kid; those memories of my mother 'secretly crying' helped me mature.

> *"Maturity doesn't come with age but begins with the acceptance of responsibility."*
>
> (Edwin Louis Cole)[2]

There was no contest; the choice was easy to make … I would give most of my earnings to Mum or simply do some shopping for what was needed. This was my contribution to the family, and such moments were pivotal in my life. At this young age, the decision was clear: I determined that my family and my children (if I ever had any) would not go through what I went through. I was going to be a man who provided! I bet some of those people who did not consider me as mature had no idea about this aspect of me. Never judge a book by its cover!

It was around this age that the most significant change in my life happened. I had gone outside to empty the trash when I bumped into a lad a few years older than me. We exchanged greetings, and I discovered that we attended the same high school and that he lived with his elder brother. Ensuing conversations revealed that he and his brother were born-again believers, and he invited me to church.

After some persuasion (and being told the church had good music), I attended a number of what appeared to be 'strange' meetings. I found it particularly strange when people started mumbling in what I considered to be some kind of weird language. But it was during one of those strange meetings that God got my attention.

That particular Sunday seemed like it was business as usual. The preacher preached, and to be honest, I cannot recall anything of what he said. Following that was the altar call – this was the time of the service where the preacher petitioned the congregation to make a commitment to follow Jesus, to become a Christian. This was something that had taken place at all the meetings I had previously attended, but I had not responded.

However, something really bizarre happened that day. As the preacher spoke, he moved a pointing finger across the congregation while saying the words, "Somebody here today needs to give their life to Jesus." Even though his hand was moving, it felt like his finger was actually pointing firmly and directly at me. To cut a long story short, I responded to his appeal and gave my life to the Lord. I believe this was in His (God's) divine timing. At that time, I did not fully grasp the significance of this change, but it was the beginning of the amazing journey of faith that I am still on today.

> *"God has perfect timing*
> *Never early, never late.*
> *It takes a little patience*
> *And it takes a lot of faith*
> *But it's worth the wait."*

(Lyrics from *Worth the Wait* by 33 Miles)[3]

My relationship with the elder brother of the lad who invited me to church has been one of key importance for well over thirty years. In him, I found a big brother and father-type figure; someone who unconditionally listened to me, understood me, encouraged me, believed in me and motivated me.

The special thing about the relationship was that it transcended into spiritual and emotional matters, the levels at which I was unhappy, disgruntled, disappointed and angry. I was very encouraged to see the truth of God's Word in Proverbs chapter 18 verse 24, which says, *"…there is a friend who sticks closer than a brother."*

Don't get me wrong; there had been other men who assumed, to a lesser or greater degree, the role of a natural 'father figure' at various stages in my life. From my position of not having a father present in my life, I did appreciate their presence and efforts to fill that void. However, the truth is that it was not easy to connect with some of them because they had their own families.

Understandably, their family was their priority, and I often felt like I was a rung or two down the ladder. I say this because you can be told that you are loved, but what is between the lines paints a slightly different picture. For me, it was the little comments, the barely noticeable gestures that seemed to, at times, speak the opposite. The reality and the main point I need you to grasp is this: even the men who meant good could only fill the father void up to a certain point.

> *"For though you might have ten thousand instructors in Christ, yet you do not have many fathers."*
>
> (1 Corinthians 4:15, NKJV)

It is one thing that natural father figures had short-comings but another to find that I had similar experiences when I came to faith. I expected better of spiritual fathers, but in the church, I found similar responses from some spiritual fathers who considered my life to be a joke. It was very painful when the people I respected, looked up to and trusted behaved in a way that depicted they never really knew me in the first place. Their attitudes demonstrated a superficial or, quite possibly, a non-existent relationship. Because of the truths I held from my experiences with natural father figures, these encounters compounded my disappointment and caused me to develop a level of distrust.

It is never pleasant when those who are supposed to nurture you hurt you instead. But glory to God, I have grown in my relationship with Him – not only as my God, but also as my heavenly Father, and I now know with certainty that He never leaves me nor forsakes me (see Deuteronomy 31:6 and Hebrews 13:5). Added to that, my heavenly Father has so graciously brought men into my life who have been the godly spiritual fathers I needed. Even though some Christian leaders hurt me emotionally, I can honestly say that I still have appreciated the time and input that each man of God has given me. We're all on a journey towards Christlikeness, and I recognise that no one is perfect, even when intentions are good.

I will take a moment to point out that not having a father around is not easy. However, it is not something to be used as a crutch or as an excuse to become deviant in life. I am sympathetic to other people who, like me, were raised by single parents. But that should never inform the choices we make nor dictate the paths we take. Take courage if this is your situation – I know people who grew up with both parents, yet had quite dire outcomes!

Remember, you cannot blame someone else. Learn to take responsibility, because it is your own choices that will make you or, indeed, break you. Due to sin, the 'blame game' is now inherently wired into human nature; if you do not believe this, then just read the third chapter of Genesis!

I read a tweet from Rick Warren that I found very simple but quite liberating: *"You start healing the moment you stop blaming."*[4] You may not be able to change the past, but you certainly can influence and change your future. Against whatever odds, determine to be one of the success stories!

"Any change, any loss,
does not make us victims.

Others can shake you, surprise you, disappoint
you, but they can't prevent you from acting,
from taking the situation you're presented with
and moving on.

No matter where you are in life, no matter what
your situation, you can always do something.

You always have a choice and the
choice can be power."

(Blaine Lee)[5]

*"Change comes with pain...
But this pain later becomes
gain. To explain it well, "no
pain, no gain"!
Endure the pain and make a
difference!"*

(Israelmore Ayivor)[1]

Chapter Three
Enduring the Pain

There is nothing like a six-year high school curriculum to get one settled into routines! However, like all school programmes, high school also came to an end, and I had to encounter the grown-up world. From childhood, I had a very strong and keen interest in aviation, so I knew from a very early age what profession I wanted to pursue. I had big plans for my life, and there was nothing wrong with that.

After my A-Levels, I successfully completed four years of Aircraft Engineering training. I also successfully attained my Aircraft Maintenance Engineer's type-rated license. Things were going well, and life was good. I got married (and I'm sure those of you who are married can attest to that fact that this in itself is a really big change), we bought a house, and a couple of years later, we decided to start a family.

The transition to parenthood was also a major change (I'll never forget when we found out that we were expecting twins – don't worry, I did not faint!). I was excited but equally apprehensive about being a father; I felt parenthood was going to be one of my biggest challenges due to the fatherhood gap in my own life. The insecurities of coming from a single-parent home started to kick in, for I believed that I wouldn't be adequate for the task. By God's grace, I learned and adapted.

Raising children in itself is an ongoing process of change. Not only did I have to adapt to the initial experience, but I also had to adjust to the changes each phase brought as the children grew – and this is still ongoing.

Everything in my life was going well until a decision was made (due to difficult economic and operational circumstances) to close down the private airline I worked for, and I was made redundant along with several dozen other people. At that moment, all my plans, the future I had envisaged and the commitments I had made seemed to unravel and go awry. Here's the **P** of what I call the **PAIN** of change!

"Pain is temporary. Quitting lasts forever."

(Lance Armstrong)[2]

In 1998, I moved to the UK hoping to get another aircraft engineering job (I am a person who tries to plan and think ahead). I was very confident that I would get a job – after all, I was well qualified and marketable.

This move was a massive change as well as a shock to the system on many levels! The cold, bitter and miserable weather was one thing. But I also had to adjust to the social and cultural differences, the different food, grasping people's accents and a whole lot more.

When I left Africa, I had been married for only two years and eight months, and my children were only three months old. The separation was a very difficult and excruciating experience, far beyond description. We were away from each other for more than a year.

I was able to see my wife regularly for she worked as a flight attendant at that time and would fly to London. However, there were gaps of several months between seeing the children. Again, this demonstrates the **PAIN** of change. In my heart, I knew it was something I had to do (because I needed to get a job and establish a base in the UK before relocating my family), but it opened up some old and very deep wounds.

I was in a lot of turmoil and anguish, drawn back to the thoughts of not knowing my father. Many times, I felt like I had abandoned my family, in particular, feeling that I had left my children fatherless the way I had been fatherless. On several nights, I would cry myself to sleep, thinking about the precious loved ones I had left behind. I wondered if this separation would create the same disconnection between myself and my family that I had experienced in my childhood. However, I had to endure the pain.

"It is never easy to endure pain nor uncomfortable situation[s].

It is [sic] seems easy to quit to avoid the pain.

If you quit you will suffer later.

It is far better to endure the pain now and enjoy later.

Life is all about endurance."

(Lailah Gifty Akita)[3]

I experienced another painful change thirteen years later. This time, it went a whole lot deeper. By that time, my wife and children had long since joined me in the UK, and life was going well. I did not envisage I would go through any more pain than what I had already been through. How wrong I was!

It was Saturday 28th May 2011, five days before my mother's sixty-fourth birthday. I had spoken to her earlier in the week, promising to call her on her birthday.

Sound engineering is amongst one of my talents, and I was at church behind the sound desk (doing a sound check in preparation of a church event). My phone rang, and I could see from the caller ID that it was my sister in Zimbabwe. My immediate assumption was that she was calling me about the surprise birthday party we were planning for Mum. I had asked her to call me that day so that we could discuss what was needed and what my financial contribution would be. I was busy at the time, so I contemplated not taking the call.

However, I had such a strong tugging within me to take the call, which I did. I said, "Hello, Jean," and someone else (a lady) said, "Sorry, it's not Jean, though this is her phone." I asked why she had my sister's phone, and she advised me that they were at the medical wing of a rehabilitation centre, not far from where my mum lived. My mother had been rushed there because she had been found inexplicably unresponsive on her bed at home after attending a wedding. A medical team were desperately trying to resuscitate her.

I was phoning Zimbabwe every five or so minutes to obtain an update, and every time I was told, "They're still trying." I was praying that my mother would not die; as someone who was now working in a clinical capacity (and the explanation for this career change is coming!), I knew that the longer the resuscitation attempts continued, the bleaker her prognosis became. After what seemed like an eternity (but realistically, maybe about twenty or so minutes later), I was able to speak to the doctor, whose words were, "I'm sorry, Mr Chikwanah, we tried all we could, but we couldn't revive your mother."

My mother had gone home to be with the Lord. One of the most significant and influential people in my life was no more.

The doctor then transferred the phone to my sister, and I think the words she said affected me the most. She said, "My brother, we were planning a birthday party, now we have to plan a funeral." I flew to Zimbabwe to arrange and deal with the funeral. The busyness and numbness of it all accompanied by the many palavers of family dynamics made me unaware of the fact that I had not grieved properly.

It was only two weeks later, as I sat on an aeroplane returning to the UK that the 'emotional freight train' hit me. As the aeroplane sped down the runway and took off, I was hit by an overwhelming sense that the events of the past days had been real, and I broke down crying, not caring who saw me, totally oblivious to my surroundings. This is difficult to explain, but I'm sure someone out there can identify with what I'm possibly failing to convey in words. Painful, right?

The pain we encounter during change will, at times, be out of our control, such as losing a loved one. At other times, the pain will be a direct result of the choices we make. But here's the thing: pain has a way of either paralysing or spurring people on. I did not allow it to stop me! If you allow the **P** of pain to become an aversion, then you'll never develop the resilience to move past it or the change it represents.

> *"Coping with pain isn't easy, but it isn't impossible either.*
>
> *If you just show a little courage and faith, you can definitely sail through."*
>
> (Unknown)

"Success is more permanent when you achieve it without destroying your principles."

(Walter Cronkite)[1]

Chapter Four

Honouring the Principles

L et's return to when I first moved to the UK. So, my plan to get an aviation job was in motion! I was offered several jobs, but at the last minute (and in spite of being more than suitably qualified), I was told I could not get a work permit because I was neither British nor from the EU.

Aircraft engineering jobs were not listed as 'critical jobs', meaning there was supposedly no shortage of personnel in that industry and the positions could be filled by British or EU citizens. That was one of the most frustrating experiences: knowing that the systems and policies of the nation I was hoping to live in dictated I could not work in an area I was passionate about and, therefore, I could not employ my skills! I wanted to live in the UK, primarily because the economic situation in Zimbabwe was deteriorating at an alarming rate and I wanted a better life for my young family.

There are certain things I have determined as absolutely essential for my **code of living**, and I believe that everyone should have a code to live by. If nothing else, at the very least, the Word of God should be a baseline. I will not go through my entire code, but I will mention just two elements and not in order of importance. The first is that I'll always do whatever job is **legal** to ensure the wellbeing of my family. If sweeping the streets (and no disrespect to those who do so) meant my family was adequately taken care of, I would have done it! The second is that **I will never live in any country illegally**.

Why? Because that would be breaking the law and dishonouring God (I will explain this in the paragraphs that follow). Also, I have seen too many people looking over their shoulders, paralysed with fear and failing to achieve their full potential because they are limited by their immigration status. From this, another **P** is evident; the pattern that directed my life through change was to honour the **PRINCIPLES**.

What are principles? I would like to define them as beliefs, sets of values or tenets that influence, guide and direct the way we think and, in turn, the way we behave, act and live. Principles are the foundations upon which life is built. Living without principles equates to what the Bible calls the foolish act of building a house on the sand. Sand is unstable and liable to shift – anything built on it is unstable. On the contrary, principles are like a bedrock – reliable, solid and immovable, regardless of one's circumstances (see Matthew 7:24-27). It is, therefore, wise to build upon principles.

One of the things about change is that it can create desperation. However, desperation should never make you move the goalposts, and principles must always trump compromise. What you compromise to keep (or get), you will lose!

> *"Policies are many,*
> *Principles are few.*
> *Policies will change,*
> *Principles never do."*
>
> (John C. Maxwell)[2]

Let us look at the guidance from two passages of scripture regarding principles:

Psalms 119:11 (NKJV) says, *"Your word I have hidden in my heart, that I might not sin against You."*; to make this simple, I'd put it as declaring, "God, what You say stands, and I'll do whatever You say and will not do what You say I shouldn't do."

Deuteronomy 6:16 (NKJV) says, *"'You shall not tempt the Lord your God...'"* According to 1 Corinthians 10:9, one of the sins that kept the Israelites out of the Promised Land was tempting God.

It is clear that, for the believer, God's Word should be the **ultimate, if not the only, plumb line** of how we live.

Don't expect God to bless you when you're violating the law – that's tempting God! A lot of the time, the reason people get into trouble is simply that they have failed to work the principles. **Principles work**.

I have often said to my children and to other people: "A shortcut is not always a shortcut." In fact, I have renamed some so-called shortcuts 'longcuts'. Why? Because, at times, what appears to be a shortcut diverts us far away from what could have possibly been a quicker (though inconvenient) way.

It is this aversion to inconvenience that causes people to try and 'buck the system' – that is, they end up doing things that are against the rules. We live in such a fast-lane, quick-fix society where following due processes and the discipline of doing things the right way seems to be a way of life that has either been lost totally or, if not lost, it is being eradicated rapidly from people's lives.

My pastor and mentor, Bishop Gerri Di Somma, frequently says: "Respect God's standard of truth; expect God's standard of blessing!" That's a very clear call and challenge to live the principles through and through. Even when you get things wrong, do not hide; instead, return to the **principle** of repentance itself!

"A man who stands for nothing
will fall for anything."

(Malcolm X)[3]

"There is no heavier burden than an unfulfilled potential."

(Charles M. Schulz)[1]

Chapter Five
Discovering Your Potential

How many know that a pity party is easy when things are not working out? Please understand that I am not discounting the difficulties people have faced and may still be facing. However, at some point, we have to move forward. Self-pity, after a while, is a way of endorsing stagnation and inaction. During the difficult times I encountered due to change, I had the option of sitting and wallowing in my misery – and to be honest, I did my share of it.

However, I had to make another choice, and that was to stop the wallowing. I realised that I had to break out of the tendency that we have as human beings to park ourselves and camp at the place of our misfortune. Unfortunately, it is a reality of life that undesirable things will happen. We need not blame any person, system or circumstance; rather, we need to fight for our success and our dreams.

For those who have been waiting, here is the explanation I promised for my career change from aircraft engineering to nursing! On the basis of honouring the **P** of the **principles**, as mentioned in the previous chapter, I did some research while seeking God for a way forward.

I discovered that the UK had a serious shortage of qualified registered nurses (and it still has) and that a qualification in this clinical field would open the door for me to obtain a work permit and work legally! It was like I heard within me a prompting from God saying, "You have the capacity to learn, you have a brain ... use it."

Understand that change dictates a new way of doing things. To put it biblically, *"Do not put new wine into old wineskins – there will be loss and no progress."* (Mark 2:22, paraphrased). So, I went to university, studied for three years and obtained my Registered Mental Health Nurse qualification with distinction. Subsequently, I studied further in various related areas. For instance, I studied for and qualified with a Master of Laws degree in healthcare law, which opened the door for me to work as a Mental Health Law Practitioner. The **P** that sustained me at that point in my journey of change was that I realised **I had** God-given **POTENTIAL**. Added to that, I realised that I had to **utilise** that potential.

> *"You have the potential to be*
> *anything you want."*
>
> (Fran Watson)[2]

Joseph was given two dreams as a boy, and just like him, we all have dreams in some shape or form. That is potential. Having a dream is always a good starting point, and Joseph's dreams appeared to point him towards a life of authority and influence. Similarly, my aircraft engineering career held the prospects of a good life.

In his enthusiasm, Joseph shared his dreams with his family – some may call it foolishness or fate, but whatever the case may be, this choice appeared 'on the surface' to cost him dearly. Why did it cost him? Because not everyone celebrated his potential.

His brothers already detested him, perceiving him to be the arrogant favoured one. His dreams (his potential), which painted a picture of them bowing in subservience to him, added insult to injury. What was their solution? The brothers sold him, and Joseph found himself face to face with the reality of change. From being the favourite beloved son, he soon became a slave in a foreign land (read Genesis chapter 37). What a change! Did this change bring immediate success? No!

Let me say that, sometimes, it's not wise to share certain things with others; there are those who will acknowledge your potential and support you, and there are some who will try to abort and destroy your potential through discouraging words and other means. When I was prompted to utilise my potential in another professional capacity, it was only my wife, immediate family and my inner circle of friends who knew what I was doing. However, it must also be said that we should be very sensitive to the Holy Spirit's warnings because even a so-called inner circle of friends can be treacherous. Remember, Jesus had such an inner circle, and it contained Judas!

> *"We should always be careful whom we share our dreams and aspirations with. Not everybody will share your enthusiasm…"*
>
> (Timothy L. Brinkley)[3]

For Joseph, rather than walking in authority and receiving honour from his brothers and father as his dreams foretold, life did not initially roll out a red carpet or serve him the silver platter. As a matter of fact, he spent time scrubbing the red carpets others walked on and polishing silver platters for others to eat from. He had to endure. And he had to believe – not just in himself, but also in the Almighty God who had planted that seed in him. His dreams still carried **potential** regardless of the adverse circumstances he was facing.

In fact, if you think about it, God has put potential in **EVERYTHING**. It's just down to perspective to see it! In Genesis 1:28, we see: *"God blessed them; and God said to them, 'Be fruitful and multiply, and fill the earth, and subdue it; and rule over the fish of the sea and over the birds of the sky and over every living thing that moves on the earth.'"*

Let's review the keywords that God spoke to mankind (male and female) after creating them: *be fruitful, multiply, fill the earth, subdue it, rule over it.* These directives are short, but they are very profound because they carry and declare the message that God has hardwired **potential** into mankind!

There is no one, absolutely no one, who is devoid of potential … and that means you, too! The devil would love to blind you to this precious truth. Don't let him rob you any longer; recognise that you have potential within you.

I love watching programmes about nature and wildlife, and I'll never forget the show I saw that explained that seeds can lie dormant, even for decades, until the right conditions exist for them to germinate. In that state of dormancy, they still carry their potential to produce. At times, change is one of the catalysts that wakes us up to the potential of what is within or around us. It did in me!

> *"Every human being has the potential for greatness."*
>
> (Robert Foster Bennett)[4]

When I was at school, I learned a lot about 'potential energy'. When something has potential energy, it has stored within it the capacity, the power or the ability to release that energy to do something. It means that when presented with the opportunity or the right circumstances, that potential is released.

A battery is something that has potential energy. At face value, a battery looks unimpressive and rather nondescript; however, do not judge it by its unassuming appearance, because its potential is only released, utilised and appreciated when it is connected to an appliance. The right conditions matter for the potential within to be realised and released.

The crises brought about by change should always be great eye-openers to the potential we hold. For Joseph, the crisis was losing his status with no prospects of regaining it. For Moses, the crisis was the prospect of returning to Egypt and facing Pharaoh after having fled Egypt as a murderer. For David, the crisis was facing Goliath. And in my case, the crisis was the change brought about by redundancy. However, in such situations, we have a choice: we can hide and avoid the crisis, or we can do something about it.

When the demands of change or crises present themselves, it's easy to ignore, deny or fight against our untapped potential, the very thing that could be released to change our situation or steer it in an entirely different direction. By submitting my situation to God, He helped me to look deeper within, and I was able to see the **potential** for turning around what could have been a disastrous situation.

*"Potential is a priceless treasure, like gold.
All of us have gold hidden within, but we have
to dig to get it out."*

(Joyce Meyer)[5]

As examples, we can look at the two other men I've just mentioned, focussing on them **personally** as well as on the '**tools**' at their disposal. Both Moses and David had potential *within them*, and there was also potential in the things (*or tools*) around them. Their outlooks, however, were entirely different.

Let's start with Moses. He had been raised in the palace of Egypt by Pharaoh's own daughter. I would like to think that he was as just as eloquent and as knowledgeable as the Egyptians – after all, he was educated in the palace as a prince and would have been taught the Egyptian practices at an even higher level than the average person. The Bible tells us in Acts 7:22 (AMP) that *"…Moses was **educated** in all the **wisdom** and **culture of the Egyptians**, and he was a **man of power in words and deeds**."*

He was full of **potential**, yet he either doubted it or was fearful. I say this because *"… Moses pleaded with the Lord, 'O Lord, **I'm not very good with words. I never have been, and I'm not now**, even though you have spoken to me. I get tongue-tied, and my words get tangled.'"* (Exodus 4:10, NLT).

"Fear and self-doubt have always been the greatest enemies of human potential."

(Brian Tracy)[6]

And what of the shepherd's staff (the **tool**) that Moses had carried in his hand for many years? It was just a stick to him. He never saw his staff beyond that. Yet, it is the same stick mentioned in Exodus 4:2 (NIV): *"Then the Lord said to him, 'What is that in your hand?' 'A staff,' he replied."* Moses did not see the **potential** in his staff.

However, God gave him a different perspective by performing many signs and wonders through that very staff. It was stretched out over the land of Egypt to start some of the plagues. It was used in the parting of the Red Sea. It was used to strike the rock that produced water in the wilderness. There are too many scriptures to mention them individually, but you can read chapters 4 through to 10 of Exodus to see how Moses eventually utilised the tools God had given him to great effect.

The key thing I want you to see is this: by the time Israel entered into battle with the Amalekites, Moses' perspective regarding the **potential** of his staff had radically changed. As the Bible tells us, *"So Moses said to Joshua, 'Choose men for us and go out, fight against Amalek. Tomorrow I will station myself on the top of the hill with the **staff of God** in my hand.'"* (Exodus 17:9). With God's perspective, the staff once considered to be just a nondescript stick was now seen to carry huge **potential as the staff of God**!

Let us now turn to David. The odds seemed stacked against him because no one saw his potential. When the prophet Samuel was looking to anoint the next king of Israel, David almost seemed an afterthought, even to his own father who had to be asked before he remembered, "Hey, there's another son of mine out there!" (1 Samuel 16:1-13). In 1 Samuel chapter 17, David is seen as being inexperienced in battle. He is undermined and derided by his own brothers, by King Saul and even Goliath himself (see verses 28, 33 and 43).

But David knew the God-given **potential** that was **within him**, and this is clearly demonstrated by his confident responses:

"'Don't worry about this Philistine,' David told Saul. 'I'll go fight him!'

'...I have been taking care of my father's sheep and goats ... When a lion or a bear comes to steal a lamb from the flock, I go after it with a club and rescue the lamb from its mouth. If the animal turns on me, I catch it by the jaw and club it to death. I have done this to both lions and bears, and I'll do it to this pagan Philistine, too, for he has defied the armies of the living God!'

David replied to the Philistine, '...I come to you in the name of the Lord of Heaven's Armies – the God of the armies of Israel, whom you have defied. Today the Lord will conquer you, and I will kill you and cut off your head.

And then I will give the dead bodies of your men to the birds and wild animals, and the whole world will know that there is a God in Israel!" (1 Samuel 17:32, 34-36, 45-46, NLT).

> **"If you could see the potential within you it would amaze you to see all that you are capable of being."**
>
> (Catherine Pulsifer)[7]

Right there, some people would be offended and bent out of shape. They would interpret David's remarks as conceit and arrogance. However, that was not arrogance; it was the language of faith coming out of a young man who knew his potential **in God**! It is by knowing our potential that, like David, we can realise *"...the urgency of seeing both the reality of the moment and the opportunity God has given."*[8]

It takes such a high level of boldness and confidence to make such declarations as David did. To be able to do that, one must be absolutely sure of where they stand. This same level of surety is seen in the Apostle Paul. Here is his firm, clear and unwavering assertion: *"I can do all things [which He has called me to do] through Him who strengthens and empowers me [to fulfill His purpose – I am self-sufficient in Christ's sufficiency; I am ready for anything and equal to anything through Him who infuses me with inner strength and confident peace.]"* (Philippians 4:13, AMP).

Paul was not boasting. Indeed, he had a lot to boast about for he had a very impressive resume (or CV) **in the flesh**. He said about himself: *"...circumcised the eighth day, of the nation of Israel, of the tribe of Benjamin, a Hebrew of the Hebrews; as to the Law, a Pharisee; as to zeal, a persecutor of the church; as to the righteousness which is in the Law, found blameless."* (Philippians 3:5-6). Prior to knowing Jesus, Paul's confidence was in his own abilities, as shown from these verses, but following his conversion, the **potential** he carried was **backed by God** and not his ability, as shown from the declaration he made in Philippians 4:13!

Back to David! With regards to the **tools** at his disposal, other people (which may very well be the entire army of Israel and possibly Goliath and the Philistines) could have bathed, drank from or even crossed the brook from which David took the stones he would use. I'm sure they saw mere stones, but David (with God's perspective) saw in those stones a weapon with the **potential** to kill Goliath.

"Don't set limits on your unlimited potential."

(Unknown)

1 Samuel 17 verses 40 and 49-50 reads:

"He ... chose for himself five smooth stones from the brook, and put them in the shepherd's bag which he had, even in his pouch, and his sling was in his hand; and he approached the Philistine.

And David put his hand into his bag and took from it a stone and slung it, and struck the Philistine on his forehead. And the stone sank into his forehead, so that he fell on his face to the ground.

*Thus David prevailed over the Philistine with a **sling and a stone**, and he struck the Philistine and killed him; but there was no sword in David's hand."*

There are two very powerful points I want to make from the verses we have just read. I wonder if you noticed them – both are things I had not quite grasped or fully appreciated until writing this book.

The first point is that it took just one stone to kill Goliath, not all five that David selected. This should teach us not to undermine or underestimate even one bit of the potential that is in or around us, no matter how small it seems and no matter how big the obstacle we face.

Sometimes, God uses the small things we have to release the greatest potential; that way, we cannot boast! Did Jesus not say we need to have faith like a tiny mustard seed, through which we can do much, such as speaking to deep-rooted trees and they will be uprooted? (see Luke 17:6). When faced with change, it takes faith to release our potential.

The second point is that David had no sword in his hand. In those times, a sword was usually the conventional or standard-issue equipment for war. King Saul had even tried to give David his own equipment.

I'm glad David didn't use it – I can speculate that Saul would have tried to take the glory by shouting, "He used **my** sword; **we** killed Goliath."

After David had struck Goliath with that one stone, he decapitated him. And what did he use? A sword. To be clear, it was Goliath's own sword. 1 Samuel 17:51, NKJV says: *"Therefore David ran and stood over the Philistine, took his sword and drew it out of its sheath and killed him, and cut off his head with it."*

Make no mistake: when the enemy of your soul comes to battle, he means business and is well prepared to annihilate you. Sometimes, the tools that the enemy brings, such as adverse circumstances, loss and misfortune, are the very things that will work to your advantage. In David's situation, it was Goliath's tool – the thing he had brought to destroy David – that sealed his own fate. God did things in an unconventional way by using an unconventional individual with unconventional tools.

What talent, gifting, skill and ability do you have within you? What resources (tools) are around you? May the God of heaven open your eyes to see the potential within you and around you!

"Your talent [potential] is God's gift to you. What you do with it is your gift back to God."

(Leo F. Buscaglia)[9]

*"Your priorities are
your character."*

(Unknown)

Chapter Six

Knowing Your Priorities

After my nursing training at university, I obtained a work permit, then a few years later, I gained my indefinite leave to remain status, allowing me to legally live and work in the UK. I was working in London, where my rise in the National Health Service (NHS) was quite rapid. Professionally, I was making it again, but spiritually and relationally, I was struggling.

Now, I am not one to throw out the baby with the bathwater. The place my family and I were fellowshipping in London was a branch of the church we had attended and had been a part of in Africa for many years. I had been a member of the London branch since March 1998, and my wife and the twins joined the church when they arrived in the UK in late 1999. We learned a lot of things there, but a time came when my wife and I felt that it could not remain our spiritual home. God was leading us in a different direction that would meet many of our needs and desires.

Without going into too much detail, God led us to Carmel City Church in Bristol. Before we moved, my wife and I met with the man who was our pastor at that time and informed him of our decision; we did not just leave and disappear. The parting was very amicable, and we left with our pastor's blessings. Today, we still have a very good relationship with him and his family because we followed the appropriate channels. It is always important to leave properly.

Dr Ed Cole stated, *"There are two things we do in life: We leave and we enter … How you leave one place is how you enter the next."* Leave badly, and you will also enter badly. In other words, you will bear the unsettled issues you took with you from where you came, and they will plague you where you are going! Worse still, you close the door for your return, so don't burn your bridges!

One of the things that initially came to my mind about moving to Bristol was, "Oh no, this is yet another change … leaving friends, leaving family (natural and spiritual), leaving the professional prospects of success and position." However, the fundamental question I had to ask myself was: **"Chris, what's the important thing to do right now?"** I had to make a life or death choice right there (*"…I have set before you life and death … choose life."* Deuteronomy 30:19).

Let me explain: London seemed to be promising a good life of success, rapid career progression and the like. But this was coming at a price in the form of a struggling marriage, spiritual stagnation and raising children in an environment that was having a negative impact on their behaviour. The choice was to either remain in London and fake it with the likelihood of losing the most important things (death to mine and my family's potential) or move to a place where we could be healed and restored (life). The ball was in my court. I had to make the decision. And I chose to follow God. God can only present the options, but the decision to act always rests with us.

An apt biblical example of this is found in Numbers chapters 13 and 14. God had a Promised Land for His people, the Israelites, and He pulled out all the stops to free them from Egypt because He wanted to get them there. But when the time came for them to possess that land, they refused to do so, choosing to defy God and choosing to remain in the wilderness of their comfort zone. The end results? They died in the wilderness.

Now, let's be clear about what caused that – it was their choice. They could have enjoyed the fullness of a land that flowed with milk and honey (life), but they chose a dry and barren wilderness instead (death), where ultimately, they died. It was as if inheriting what God had promised and living to God's standard was not important.

In my situation, I knew what I needed to do, and I made a choice!

Where is this all leading to? The **P** that sustained me at the phase of change I was about to encounter was that

I followed the **PRIORITIES**. The world so desperately needs people who are bold enough to stand for their priorities, people who can make bold declarations like Joshua did when he was presented with the option of jumping on the bandwagon or sticking to his priorities.

Joshua was absolutely clear about where he stood, saying, *"But as for me and my family, we will serve the Lord.'"* (Joshua 24:15, NLT). He lived his whole life knowing and following the right priorities. What was the result? He was one of only two people from his generation who did not die in the wilderness but crossed into the Promised Land (the other person being Caleb who also maintained right priorities)!

It's a fact that a lot of people have chased possessions, careers, money, etc., prioritising them over what is truly important. Sometimes, we need to ask ourselves the fundamentally important questions that the Word of God asks. I would not be surprised if scriptures that ask key and 'in-your-face' questions, such as, *"For what will it profit a man if he gains the whole world, and loses his own soul?'"* (Mark 8:36, NKJV) are ones that are the least read! Yet, how many people have supposedly 'gained the world' and paid the price in other areas of their lives? Is money, fame or fortune worth a broken marriage or living a life that is out of sync with God?

What about, *"But seek first the kingdom of God and His righteousness, and **all** these things shall be added to you.'"* (Matthew 6:33, NKJV)? We do not always like to hear or read that, do we? I left a very promising job in London (where I had been dubbed a rising star, and people had made all sorts of predictions about my upward trajectory), and I actually took a lower position by relocating to Bristol ... however, it was worth it.

> *"In order to say yes to your priorities, you have to be willing to say no to something else."*
>
> (Unknown)

It was not long when what appeared to have been lost was regained ... promotions, spiritual stability, relational soundness, children serving God, etc. – things that money cannot buy. This is not to say I'm 'there' yet, but I'm learning and choosing **day by day** not to major on the minor things and not minor on the major things. This is called knowing your **priorities**!

I firmly believe this: if you feel something is important, you'll always find a way. Likewise, if you feel it is not, you'll always find an excuse. When faced with a challenge, adjustments are vital; it is these adaptations that develop new capacities for decision making, and good priority-setting is at the top of it.

Faced with the challenge to fulfil my priorities, not only did I need to change location, but I, myself, needed to change. I had to adopt a different approach to life, and I had to think differently. There are times when it is necessary to think outside of the box and shift our paradigms to embrace what will work in a particular season and environment.

I draw upon the very wise words of General Stanley McChrystal, a former commanding officer of US and coalition forces fighting in Afghanistan, who had to be flexible and adaptable. He wrote this to describe the difference between the strategies in which he was trained and the reality of what he had to execute: *"This was not a war of planning and discipline; it was one of agility and innovation."*[2]

What was General McChrystal saying? I believe he was expressing the necessity of learning to do things differently. There are some things that are tried and tested, but there's always great scope for innovation. For example, the petrol engine is still useful, but with preserving the environment being a **priority**, new technologies are also emerging!

*"Good things happen when
you get your priorities straight."*

(Scott Caan)[3]

"People with great passion can make the impossible happen."

(Unknown)

Chapter Seven
Maintaining Your Passion

You might not appreciate why hundreds of thousands of football and other sporting fans spend millions of pounds (or whatever currency) on travelling, memorabilia and season or one-off tickets. Why do they do it? Why are they totally sold-out and so doggedly driven and spurred on by their pursuits?

This pattern of behaviour and determination is displayed and exhibited all over the world. It seems to transcend a lot of barriers and knows no race, class, creed, age or status. The CEO will rub shoulders with the janitor at a football match. Both will shout, cheer on their team and support their cause, oblivious to societal constructs. This appears to be the case regardless of whether the cause (sporting or otherwise) is worthwhile, extremely radical or flawed in its nature, purpose or outcomes.

I have asked myself the same questions pertaining to the changes I have encountered. When we moved from Zambia to Zimbabwe, something drove those who made the decision on my behalf. What was it? When I reached the age of accountability, something drove me to make the decisions I made in response to the change-related challenges I faced, irrespective of whether those changes were self-determined or triggered by circumstances beyond my own control. What drove me?

When I moved to the UK, I was driven by something yet again. In this instance, my drive could have easily been classified as survival instincts – instincts to achieve something, to care and provide for my family. I believe that was partly true. However, I also believe that there was and is another dimension to what drives a person. A lot of times, what appears to be the obvious driving force or motivating factor is not what actually spurs somebody on. Rather, this drive is being fuelled by something deeper.

Often, the tendency and pattern in life is to judge what is seen. People will often see and focus on the behaviour or action rather than the root cause of that behaviour. We can learn a lot from what I term the 'diagnostic world'. Diagnosis is important because it delves into the causative factors of a matter, and it informs and directs the outcome(s) with which to deal with whatever is at hand.

Where am I going with this? When we are faced with any sort of change or when there is a need for it, it is easy to go one of two ways. On the one hand, we may refrain from making any decisions, while on the other hand, we may make rash, knee-jerk decisions. The latter is a particularly common reaction when a person is not guided by our next **P** of change. From my own life experiences of change, I can say there is a common thread linking all the things I have mentioned that could give us an answer.

I believe it is **PASSION**.

According to Jim Collins, *"Nothing can happen without beginning with **passion**."* Citing Tod Bolsinger, Collins states, *"True urgency* [and focus] *... is centred on the **passion** and vision...* [that is instrumental to] *developing a clear conviction* [for the] *mission."* (author's emphasis).

> *"Nothing is as important as passion.*
> *No matter what you want to do with your life,*
> *be passionate."*
>
> (Jon Bon Jovi)[3]

In the face of change, it was **passion**, not survival per se, that drove me. And it continues to drive me to do what I do today.

Jesus Christ, our Lord and Saviour, saw the need for mankind to change. He knew that the penalty or price God required for man's redemption meant a lot of change for Him. The kicker is this: He also knew that some of the ones He came to save would be contemptible towards Him and reject Him (see Isaiah 53 if you do not believe me). What did He do? He still went to the cross, shedding His blood and suffering what was probably one of the most horrendous ways to die. Why? **Passion**!

During change and its challenges, we can easily embark on what we believe are solutions-focussed journeys. However, if there is no passion, we will eventually run out of steam. Therefore, we need to remain passionate about what we do and about the things that matter, as that is what will drive us along, even if those things come at a personal cost.

A note of caution here – it is under the name of 'passion' that insane things have been done. Please never confuse passion with fanaticism! According to David Gerrold, *"If a fanatic is willing to give his life for a cause, he's probably willing to give yours as well."*[4] That is the difference between fanaticism and passion. Jesus' passion for us cost Him and no one else! Be passionate, but let your passion be directed towards the right things and the right reasons!

> *"If you can't figure out your purpose, figure out your passion. For your passion will lead you right into your purpose."*
>
> (Bishop T.D. Jakes)[5]

"Purpose is what gives life a meaning."

(Richard Leider)[1]

Chapter Eight

Recognising Purpose

Change is something with which people are not always comfortable. And let's be real, change usually *is* uncomfortable – invariably, it involves the process of losing and letting go of things that we hold dear, and it involves adjusting some things we are doing and then taking on something that may seem unknown.

There's a leadership book on change that I have read called *Canoeing the Mountains* by Tod Bolsinger, and he quotes two other authors, Heifetz and Linsky, who wrote this: *"People don't resist change, per se. They resist loss."* [2] Giving up the present and the familiar can seem a loss to us, but this 'supposed loss' could be the very launching pad into a better future.

It is a reality that the processes of change will be seen as a loss if there is no clear focal point for that change. Right here, another **P** emerges; the pattern that sustained me through change was to realise and acknowledge that there was **PURPOSE** behind the change. At the time, some things I went through were painful and difficult. A good example of this is when some people outside of my inner circle of friends discovered that I had taken up nursing – they mocked me and laughed at my new career choice.

The ironic thing is this: for the many years that I was an accomplished aircraft engineer, no one (to my recollection, anyway) ever addressed me by my title – no one had ever greeted me by saying, "How is Christopher, the engineer?" Yet, after I took up nursing, certain people would greet me, "How's Christopher, the nurse?" Subtle and innocent, it seemed, but they were mocking me nonetheless. That would be enough to 'wind up' some people, and it did affect me for a while.

One might have expected that I would have received encouragement, admiration and applause for adapting and making such a bold choice that had **purpose** and not **pride** behind it! It was purpose, not pride, that enabled me to provide for my family and give them a good quality of life.

However, I have learned to take people by surprise. I'll refer to something very simple as an illustration. Have you ever been given a nickname that you disliked? What is the natural response to this? It is usually resistance and irritation! Someone is probably nodding their head right now, identifying with this experience.

> *"We won't be distracted by comparison
> if we're captivated with purpose."*
>
> (Bob Goff)[3]

That is exactly how people expect you to respond, and the greater the resistance and irritation you display, the more the nickname is rubbed in! I don't know about you, but this taught me something profound: to respond in exactly the opposite way! This blows people's minds and frustrates the very thing they are trying to achieve.

Initially, my self-esteem was low, and I would feel down at times, but I knew that I was pursuing a greater **purpose** and that realisation (or rather, revelation) kept me on track. One very important thing I would like to mention at this point is that **people can be extremely fickle** – this means they change frequently. I am certain, beyond any shadow of a doubt, that the same people who mocked me and laughed at me for turning to nursing as a way of making a living so that I could provide for my family (**MY PURPOSE AS A MAN**) would have been the very same people whose derision I would have faced had I failed in that respect.

The moral of the story? You can't please people! In fact, my purpose for immigrating to the UK was not survival (as I believed it to be at the time); behind the scenes, God had a **GREATER PURPOSE**. This is put across very well in Proverbs 19:21 (NIV): *"Many are the* *plans in a person's heart, but it is the Lord's **purpose** that prevails.* " So simple and yet so profoundly true!

Your purpose will pull you out of the rut if you know it and pursue it. Purpose jump starts you and continues to spur you on in life. Why? Because it is God-given. The Bible says *"He has saved us and called us to a holy life – not because of anything we have done but because of his own **purpose** and grace. This grace was given us in Christ Jesus before the beginning of time."* (2 Timothy 1:9, NIV).

Having and fulfilling purpose should not be hard, because firstly, it is a God-ordained disposition, and secondly, His grace is present to help you realise and subsequently fulfil that purpose. Facing change and experiencing difficulties should not distract you; instead, they should energise you, because you still have a purpose. Your purpose should be the forward, not the reverse gear of your life.

My work in the mental health and health law services has brought me into contact with many people who have encountered varying difficult and challenging situations. Some of these people have experienced similar things to me, such as redundancy, and the only solution they could conceive was to attempt committing suicide – sadly, for some, successfully.

> *"For the secret of human existence does not consist of living, merely, but in what one lives for."*
>
> (Fyodor Dostoyevsky)[4]

Please hear my heart; I am not underplaying people's pain, situations or circumstances. However, I believe that they were driven to suicide for one primary reason: they could not see beyond their situation, so they had lost their **hope and purpose**.

Do not ever make your situation, no matter how painful or difficult, become greater than your purpose!

Mankind is prone to self-destructive tendencies when hope and purpose are lost. Purpose and hope are like the wind in the sails of life, the thermal currents upon which we soar. On this matter, we can glean wisdom from King Solomon, the wisest man to live. He was able to recognise that *"Hope [**purpose**] deferred makes the heart sick, but desire fulfilled is a tree of life."* (Proverbs 13:12).

Be sustained by hope, which is a confident expectation. God has so clearly said, *"'For I know the plans I have for you,' says the Lord. 'They are plans for good and not for disaster, to give you a **future** and a **hope**.'"* (Jeremiah 29:11, NLT). That hope, dear readers, is purpose! Go on and live that purpose. Get back in the saddle of life.

> *"If we have our own WHY in life, we shall get along with almost any how."*
>
> (Friedrich Nietzsche)[5]

"Character's who you are under pressure, not who you are when everything's fine."

(Dr Lance Sweets, fictional character from Bones TV series)[1]

Chapter Nine

Resisting the Pressure

The crucial point in my life occurred when I came to the end of myself and became more motivated by the desire to benefit my family. That's what love does — it seeks the benefit of others at the expense of self. I stopped being driven by my own selfish pride, and I determined that living successfully (spiritually and relationally) was going to be my primary focus and motivating factor, not my status, titles or other people's opinions.

Some of you may not understand the significance of this, especially if you have never lived in a place like Africa. Unbeknown to many people in western countries, African society is highly competitive. So much so that who you are is measured by the yardstick of your title, education and so forth. In essence, it's a society where status is everything. And the thing is this … some people will do anything to get ahead of the pack!

Since I was already a very self-conscious person, this phenomenon did not help me when I was growing up. I have already mentioned that I was brought up by a single parent and that we were poor (yet, my late mother did her best to provide for us and educate us. Education in Africa is not free like it is in the UK. Added to that, there is no such thing as state benefits!).

Because of my family's situation, both socially and economically, some people (including some we considered to be family) did not believe that my sisters and I would ever amount to anything. The result was that I believed I always had a point to prove. However, I had to grow up when change came, which brings me to the next **P**. In all the changes I faced, I developed the capacity to handle **PRESSURE**.

> *"The fear of human opinion disables; trusting in GOD protects you from that."*
>
> (Proverbs 29:25, MSG)

Whenever you are faced with the pressure to do something or to look the part, ask yourself, "Am I doing this for what is important to me? Or am I doing this for what is important to others?" These two questions are important because pressure has two dimensions: the first dimension is that pressure is healthy in certain circumstances, and the second dimension is that pressure can be destructive. The point? When you are facing any type of change, the pressure you experience will either be healthy or destructive, depending on how you respond to it.

Let me explain the first dimension from my own experiences of change. When I was made redundant, I was under a great deal of pressure. It was the pressure to be a responsible man who provided for his family. That kind of pressure I consider to be normal because that's really what every husband and father should do – provide! To achieve this, I had to first find my own equilibrium. Once I had obtained that, I then had to learn to resist the pressures of pride and status, which meant not performing for other people or trying to live according to their standards.

When handled properly, and when applied correctly, this first dimension of pressure can bring the best out of people. Some people have been known to produce their best in pressurised situations! Are diamonds not the result of intense pressure?!

> *"A diamond is a chunk of coal that did really well under pressure."*
>
> (Henry Kissinger)[2]

Conversely, if pressure is not handled properly or not applied to one's life in an appropriate way, it can be very destructive. This is the second dimension of pressure. What do I mean? When the pressure you are under is to appease the outside world, it will upset your equilibrium and cause you to crumble. Why do you think some athletes end up taking illegal substances, such as steroids, to win medals? It could be argued that there is an element of greed involved in their actions, but I suggest that this greed is born out of an unhealthy **pressure** to perform and to live the glitzy life of fame and fortune – to have the success they have seen in other people's lives!

In such instances, pressure can cause you to lose your identity and individuality and lead you to be constantly chasing other people's dreams, objectives, expectations and aspirations. Ultimately, it makes you irrational. What do I mean by that? The only reason you will succumb to the pressure to be someone you are not is that you believe less of yourself than you should. And the only reason you chase other people's dreams is that you believe they are better than you. This is irrational because God made you exactly as you are; you cannot be someone else, and neither can they be you – God made the best you!

It is this second dimension of pressure that can cause you (as it has so frequently caused others) to bend over backwards so as to fit into the environment, circumstances, societal dictates and the demands and expectations of the people around you. We must realise that this type of pressure breeds conformity. That is why we're so clearly instructed by the Word: *"…do not be conformed to this world…"* (Romans 12:2).

Keeping up with the Joneses is not running your own race. When I reached the crucial point of my life, my eyes were opened to see that I had danced to the tune of too many other people's songs, and I made the decision that it was time for me to WRITE MY OWN SONG and dance to that instead! The late Steve Jobs wisely said, *"Don't let the noise of others' opinions drown out your own inner voice."*[3]

There's no disputing that pressure can cause and create anxiety. Peter Steinke, a congregational systems expert, writes that we should *"...have some command over our own anxiety and some capacity not to let other people's anxiety contaminate us; that is not allow their anxiety to affect our thinking, actions, and decisions."*[4]

> *"Care about what other people think and you will always be their prisoner."*
>
> (Lao Tzu)[5]

I feel it is important at this point for me to put in a 'side thought', which I hope will not be misunderstood. Nowadays, society has begun to frown upon healthy competition (particularly in children) under the guise that it puts **pressure** on them. **This is not the pressure I am talking about!** Sadly, it is now commonplace to see prize-giving ceremonies in some schools where every child receives a prize, regardless of their actual efforts or achievements. This is what I call the 'everyone-is-a-winner mentality'.

How sad, because we are now breeding a society of people with a mentality and attitude of entitlement.

This means there are children who will grow up with no inclination to perform competitively. They will also lack resilience since they have not had the opportunity to experience and handle non-threatening pressure in their early years. Surely, we're setting them up to fail when the real pressures of life come?!

I, for one, disapprove of pushy parents. **This *is* the negative pressure I am talking about**; it should be wholly frowned upon. But there is a big difference between being a pushy parent and being a parent who directs your children to be goal-oriented. The first parent is self-centred, and the second encourages their children in pursuit of **THEIR OWN DREAMS** – and children's dreams are as unique and as individual as they are. It is in the pursuit of their dreams that your children will thrive.

Parents – do not live your life through your children by pushing them to be doctors or lawyers (or whatever) because you could not be one yourself or because it's what the Joneses and their children are doing! That is unhealthy pressure! However, if you recognise their talent or gifting, then encourage them to pursue that avenue; encouragement, not conformity, is a good form of pressure!

Remember this: we will all face change, and when faced with that change, none of us is far away from that one 'pressure-based decision' that can either make us a diamond or keep us a crumbly, dirty lump of coal!

"If you're going to let pressure stop you from fulfilling your dreams, you're robbing yourself."

(Quinton Jackson)[6]

"We have more possibilities available in each moment than we realise."

(Thích Nhất Hanh)[1]

Chapter Ten

Identifying the Possibilities

Two people in the Bible both received very similar, if not identical, pieces of news from the angel Gabriel. Both pieces of news had to do with pregnancy! In case I had lost your interest, I'm sure I have just got it back! I am talking about the Jewish priest Zechariah (who was told that his wife Elizabeth would have a child) and Mary, the yet-to-be mother of Jesus (who was told she would become pregnant and bear a son). Both accounts are found in the first chapter of the Gospel of Luke.

I would like to think that Zechariah and Elizabeth had other plans that no longer included parenthood and that Mary had plans, goals, dreams and aspirations that did not include falling pregnant out of wedlock. After all, Zechariah and Elizabeth were both advanced in years, and Mary was betrothed and must have been looking forward to what lay ahead. Then, **change happened** to them all! I believe someone can fully identify with that ... I can!

In both situations, something was triggered; these two pieces of news elicited or resulted in questions. Eerily so, the questions were almost similar, too! Zechariah's question to the angel (in Luke 1:18, NLT) was: *"'How can I be sure this will happen? I'm an old man now, and my wife is also well along in years.'"* Mary's question to the angel (in verse 34, NLT) was, *"'But how can this happen? I am a virgin.'"*

Have we not all at some point been pressed by the need to ask a question?

Mankind has always been curious and inquisitive, wanting answers and driven by the 'need to know'. The questions flow more abundantly when we do not see a logical solution or a logical way out. There is nothing wrong with curiosity or an enquiring mind. However, we need to know our limits. Why? Because some questions we ask come with certain consequences. Consider the fact that the devil was able to deceive Eve due to her curiosity and desire to know things that were off-limits. The devil promised her deeper insight, but we all know the outcome was not what he made it out to be (see Genesis 3:1-7).

> *"We live in the world our questions create."*
>
> (David Cooperrider)[2]

The truth of the matter is that we will not always have or gain the answers to some of the situations we encounter. Change can come with known and predictable outcomes. However, it can also follow a path along the unknown, and it is in these circumstances that we're not comfortable and not so willing to embrace change.

Let us now look a little deeper at the questions Zechariah and Mary asked. Zechariah's question seems to be very pertinent and very appropriate. After all, it was a priest asking, so it had to be 'in line' coming from this great man of God, right? No ... very, very wrong!

The question Zechariah asked is actually an indication of doubt. By asking, "How can I be sure it will happen?" he was, in fact, indirectly saying, "Are you sure this will this really happen? If you say so, then I need some proof." Another translation puts Zechariah's question across very well: "*How do you expect me to believe this? I'm an old man and my wife is too old to give me a child. What sign can you give me to prove this will happen?'*"(Luke 1:18, TPT). By also adding that he and his wife were old (as if God or Gabriel were unaware of this fact), he showed that he had eliminated the **P** of the **POSSIBILITY** of it ever happening.

What were the consequences of Zechariah's doubts? He became mute. For the duration of Elizabeth's pregnancy right up until the time of naming his child, Zechariah could not speak. I can only imagine that God was sitting on His throne, shaking His head at what He heard coming out of the mouth of someone who was supposed to be a great man of faith! I think

God decided that Zechariah had spoken too much and said, "Gabriel, let us shut this man up before he speaks anything else that will kill the possibilities!"

Well, have we not seen someone else do that before? Yes, we have! That was almost the same reaction Sarah gave when she overheard one of the heavenly visitors tell her husband, Abraham, that she would be holding a baby at a pre-determined time. In Sarah's case, she laughed. It was a sign of her disbelief (see Genesis 18:9-15).

"When nothing seems sure, everything is possible."

(Margaret Drabble)[3]

By contrast, Mary's question indicates she had embraced the words given, and it reflects a line of enquiry regarding the **process** (*how it will happen*) rather than one that eliminates its certainty. As a result, Mary gained a very clear perspective that the change she was facing was a God-orchestrated one.

The angel Gabriel's response to Mary was, *"'For nothing will be **impossible** with God.'"* (Luke 1:37). To put it in other words, *"**All things are POSSIBLE to those who believe!**"* (Mark 9:23, paraphrased). When I encountered all the changes in my own life, I had to stay in tune with the Spirit of God so that He could show me the **POSSIBILITIES** He had for me in the change. It was also crucial that I did not doubt Him.

When I was faced with change, I had the option to do nothing and freeze like a deer in headlights. However,

I realised that the '*que sera, sera*' (whatever will be, will be) mentality is not fit for purpose. It is a form of avoidance. Very often, it *is* good to ask questions when encountering change … so long the questions are directed to the right source, and the motivation for the asking is faith-based!

I had to seek God and ask Him to speak to me, to show me what I needed (or did not need) to do, to give me direction, to order my steps! It was during those times of seeking Him (not interrogating Him, whinging at Him or doubting Him) that He began to show me the **possibilities** that lay ahead!

I must say this … I am glad that God opened my eyes and showed me the possibilities and that I embraced and pursued them. And quite frankly, I don't care what anyone thinks as long as God is in what I'm doing. Do you think Zechariah and Elizabeth did not face any stigma, having a child in their old age? I'm sure some people would see them and wonder if John was their grandson instead of their son. Or do you think that tongues did not wag when Mary was pregnant? However, that did not matter. In both cases, these people were living out God's possibilities and were in the process of fulfilling destiny.

> "You must find the place inside yourself
> where nothing is impossible."
>
> (Deepak Chopra)[4]

God always reveals possibilities for any time, any place and in anything. The principle is that everything you set your hand to will prosper. "'*The Lord will guarantee a blessing on* **everything** *you do and will fill your storehouses with grain. The Lord your God will bless you in the land he is giving you.*'" (Deuteronomy 28:8, NLT).

The use of the word 'everything' is very significant and deliberate. It means precisely that … EVERYTHING! The problem is that people are limited by their thinking. We tend to put boundaries and borders regarding where we think God should work, how He should work and when He should work. As long as God is there, there are unlimited and unfathomable possibilities. That's the mindset I had to adopt in my times of change. I had to break out of my familiar frame of reference and acknowledge that God is beyond my 'aircraft engineering'.

I found this very beautiful and powerful quote online, which says, *"Always open your mind to the* **possibilities** *that may be hiding behind the inconvenience of change."*[5]

"Instead of thinking outside the box, get rid of the box."

(Deepak Chopra)[6]

"Position yourself well enough and circumstances will do the rest."

(Mason Cooley)[1]

Chapter Eleven

Acknowledging Your Positioning

God is a good God. Earlier, we saw that God has declared: "'...*I know the thoughts that I think towards you ... thoughts of peace and not of evil, to give you a future and a hope.*'" (Jeremiah 29:11, NKJV).

This scripture reveals the nature of God as a Father who has not left our lives to chance. God does not do 'random'. Everything God does is purposeful and by meticulous design. In my own life, I could not always see God's plans, especially during times of change. However, as I took the time to reflect and write this book, it became more and more apparent that God has always had His hand upon my life.

One does not need too much evidence to see God's handprint on all the changes that I went through. The move from Zambia to Zimbabwe, the move from Zimbabwe to the United Kingdom, the change of professions, moving from London to Bristol; the list could go on and on. In all of this, I mostly saw what I thought to be the 'ability of Christopher' to plan, strategise and think his way out of a problem. But now, I do not believe this to be the case – I'm not that clever. Let us look at it.

The move to Zimbabwe resulted in my salvation. The move to London exposed my unhealthy drive to succeed and prove a point, which had almost blinded me to the spiritual and relational stagnation I was in. The move to Bristol resulted in me connecting with people who motivated, inspired and challenged me, and it also led to me being planted in a ministry that God used to restore me spiritually, emotionally, maritally and in many other respects. I do not have to worry about my children being drunk somewhere in the gutter … they are serving God! And I now teach others the principles of God's Word, equipping and encouraging them to live successful lives.

I hope the picture is clear on this matter. Not even at my best could I have achieved or accomplished any of this. God is very deliberate about when and where HE places people. This **P** is what I call the **POSITIONING** of change!

Never believe the expression, *'The devil is in the detail'*; I prefer to say, *'**God is in the detail!**'* Why can I confidently say this? Well, from the very beginning when mankind was created, God demonstrated that He is into detail, especially when it comes to positioning.

"God will put you where He wants you even if no one thinks you deserve the position."

(Unknown)

What was one of the key things God did after creating the first man? Let's read: *"Then the Lord God formed man of dust from the ground, and breathed into his nostrils the breath of life; and man became a living being. The Lord God **planted a garden toward the east, in Eden**; and **there He placed the man** whom He had formed."* (Genesis 2:7-8). The statement, *'and there He placed the man'* speaks so clearly of **positioning**!

Let us have a look at another example. In Exodus 23:31, God declared this: *"'I will **fix your boundary** from the Red Sea to the sea of the Philistines, and from the wilderness to the River Euphrates…'"* Furthermore, the Bible says that *"'…and He made from one man every nation of mankind to live on all the face of the earth, **having determined** their appointed times and **the boundaries of their habitation**.'"* (Acts 17:26).

God's positioning, through whatever circumstances, will always bring blessings. I like the picture portrayed in Psalm 1; it talks about the man who is bringing forth his fruit in season, his leaf is not withering and whatever he does prospers! This man is productive. Why? Because he is *"…like a tree planted by the rivers of water."* (verse 3, NKJV). I will take poetic license and say it this way: "He is a tree firmly **POSITIONED** by the rivers of water!"

I believe there is a reason why God moved Abram from his people: to position him so He could broaden his mindset. He moved Israel (Jacob) and his family to Egypt to position them so they could grow, gain skills and get wealth (though their suffering could easily hide that fact!). What of getting the nation of Israel out of Egypt? They now had the wealth, prosperity and skills needed to go and fulfil their destiny at the **place** God had appointed for them many centuries earlier! All of this was positioning, positioning, positioning!

For a while, I believed that God moved me from where I was so that I could have a better economic and social lifestyle. How wrong I was! God moved me to position me for what He wanted to achieve and perform for me, in me and through me. God's positioning was so that my SOUL, first and foremost, could prosper, and out of that would flow everything else that I needed. But I first needed to be in POSITION!

Let me be clear about something – in all you do, be led and guided by the Spirit of God. Why? **Because each person's circumstances are different, and so, God's direction(s) will be different**. The fact that I was led to move and be positioned in the UK does not necessarily mean that you have to take a similar path. I say this because there are people who have remained in Zimbabwe and succeeded and prospered where they are.

In Genesis 12:1-3, we see that it was God who told Abram to leave his country and go to a land that He would show him. That physical positional change was required to bring about the blessings and prosperity of God. Interestingly, it was the same God who, in Genesis 26:2-3, told Isaac (Abraham's son), not to move to Egypt but to remain in the land that He would tell him, and God also prospered him where he was positioned.

Notice something: Abram's instruction was to LEAVE and GO to a country God would SHOW him, while Isaac's instruction was to REMAIN in the land God would TELL him. My view is this: although both men needed to be in position, Abram needed a physical transition and Isaac needed a mental transition. This tells us that God will speak to different people through different means to achieve the same result. Furthermore, I want you to understand that 'positioning' is not restricted to geographical relocation.

God may very well want you to reposition physically (geographically). However, have you thought that God might want you to reposition mentally, educationally, intellectually, relationally, professionally or emotionally? Sometimes, it is the repositioning of our attitude (easier said than done) that God wants.

Over the years, I've needed to reposition in many aspects other than geographically. I've had to reposition how I saw myself, and what I believed and thought about myself, for instance. This has meant changing my mentality from being a victim to a victor and transitioning from feeling disadvantaged to seeing myself as having opportunities equal to everyone.

Whatever the case may be, get into position, and let that position be determined by God!

A final thought for this chapter: let us learn to see change as a tool that God uses to position us ready for Him to accomplish something in us, even though we may not necessarily be seeing the bigger picture at the time.

"Your positioning will greatly influence your perspective."

(Christopher Chikwanah Snr)

"I thank God for protecting me from what I thought I wanted and blessing me with what I didn't know I needed."

(Unknown)

Chapter Twelve

The Protection of Change

We have become very reliant on technology and on computers to achieve many tasks. Everything we need is just a few clicks away, and sometimes, just one click. With this readily accessible technology comes great ease but also great risks.

Technology is not static. Each year, it changes and improves when new software programmes are created and new updates are made available. Correspondingly, there is also a growing threat from those who seek to disrupt this technology through viruses or hacking. As the technology changes, so do the threats, and so, anti-virus protection and security measures are also updated in response to these changing threats.

Just as there are technological changes, we also have to acknowledge that life is not static. Things are changing every day. We need to be alert to the changes, but equally, able to see how those changes impact our lives. We need to discern the times, like the sons of Issachar, who were considered intuitive regarding God's timing.

The enemy is always scheming in the background, seeking how to trip you up, infect you and, ultimately, destroy your life. He does this by altering your circumstances and creating an environment conducive to your destruction. However, he does not blatantly stand there showing you the threat. The devil will poison you one drop at a time until he has fully incapacitated you.

Does not the Bible warn us about the devil? It clearly tells us he is the thief who comes to steal, to kill and to destroy. The good news is that we are not only warned about the threat, but we are also given the solution. There is a counter-plan in place ... Jesus has come that we can have life and have it more abundantly (John 10:10)!

When reflecting on this scripture and on the changes in my life, I realised there was another **P** in operation, and that was **PROTECTION**. Through following God's leading, change brought His **protection**.

Just as circumstances change, God uses change in your life to empower you to be able to face the new challenges and circumstances that lie ahead. When I faced and went through change, it was not always easy to accept the changes. Try packing your bags and moving to another country while leaving your family behind – it's very inconvenient! However, I'm really glad I did it.

*"He [God] holds success in store for the upright,
he is a shield to those whose walk is blameless."*

(Proverbs 2:7, NIV)

What I left behind may have been hard to leave, but God knows the future. It was not long after I left Zimbabwe that its economy further spiralled downwards to one of the highest inflation levels any country in the world has ever known.

Through the crisis of change, and by moving to the UK, I found myself in a country with the strongest currency in the world. At that time, the exchange rate of the British pound to the Zimbabwean dollar was becoming quite alarming. Remember earlier on I indicated that my wife and I had taken out a mortgage shortly before I was made redundant? Well, due to Zimbabwe's declining economy and the strong UK currency, we were able to fully pay off our mortgage in less than two years. If I had not faced change, I would have probably remained in Zimbabwe, and it would have taken us a lot longer to clear the mortgage.

I visited Zimbabwe several times after moving to the UK, and it was devastating to see and experience some of the hardships people were facing, such as queuing for several hours to buy a few litres of fuel or queuing to buy even the most basic of commodities like bread, milk and sugar. Would you or anyone else deny that what I saw as a crisis of change was indeed God's hand moving me and positioning me in a place of **protection**?

Let us look at the life of Joseph again. When Joseph ended up in Egypt as a slave, he endured some hard times, and I'm sure he did not appreciate the change from being his father's favourite (*"Now Israel loved Joseph more than all his children, because he was the son of his old age. Also he made him a tunic of many colors."* Genesis 37:3, NKJV) to being at the bottom of the pile.

But what happened? Joseph was eventually promoted to the second-highest position of authority in Egypt – we can see Pharaoh himself saying to Joseph, *"'You shall have charge over my house, and all my people shall be governed according to your word and pay respect [to you with reverence, submission, and obedience]; only in [matters of] the throne will I be greater than you [in Egypt].' Then Pharaoh said to Joseph, 'See, I have set you [in charge] over all the land of Egypt.'"* (Genesis 41:40-41, AMP).

There are two very important questions that need to be asked regarding Joseph being positioned in Egypt. Firstly, how did Joseph attain his promotion? And secondly, what did his promotion accomplish?

To answer the first question, we need to look at what is said of the sons of Issachar. We are told in 1 Chronicles 12:32 that *"...the sons of Issachar, [were] men who understood the times, with knowledge of what Israel should do..."* This tells us something that seems to be parallel to Joseph's life. Joseph was able to discern the times by God's gift of interpreting dreams.

I believe this also relates to my experiences. I had an urgency and restlessness in my spirit that things were changing in Zimbabwe, which, with hindsight, I can only call **discerning the times** by God's Spirit.

*"Be careful about rushing God's timing…
You never know who or what He is protecting
you or saving you from."*

(Unknown)

To answer the second question, we need to look at the advice Joseph gave to Pharaoh. In Genesis 41:25-36, Joseph paints a very clear picture for Pharaoh, telling him of the hard times ahead. But Joseph does not just give Pharaoh the bad news (as a side note, there are people in life who are very good at painting bleak pictures but are never prepared to be a part of the solution – Joseph was not like that); he also tells Pharaoh that there is a solution, and he sells his plan well, sealing it by telling Pharaoh that his advice is *"'…so that the land will not perish during the famine.'"* (Genesis 41:36).

To use modern-day language, Joseph (through God) was actually providing Pharaoh with what could equate to an insurance policy or a savings plan. The purpose of insurance and savings is to ensure our protection, comfort and provision for the future.

Joseph confirms this when he later told his brothers, *"As for you, you meant evil against me, but God meant* *it for good in order to bring about this present result, to preserve [**protect**] many people alive. So therefore, do not be afraid; I will provide for you and your little ones.'"* (Genesis 50:20-21).

Just like the sons of Issachar, Joseph had God's insight to know what needed to be done in any particular situation. This resulted in **protection** for Joseph – he was protected from starvation, and not only was he protected from this fate, but so was the whole of Egypt and the rest of the world, including the very people who sold him into slavery.

Again, I believe that this applies to my journey of change. How? As I mentioned, even before I was made redundant, I had started to sense or **discern** that change was on the way and that things were changing in Zimbabwe. I seemed to know that I should prepare to transition. That transitioning came through embracing the change I did not necessarily want but knew I needed.

What did it accomplish? Well, what the enemy meant for evil turned out to be the very **protection** needed for me, my household and many others. Order was re-established in my life ... maritally, relationally, spiritually, and in other areas. The 'Chikwanah family land' did not perish, and a lot of other people have benefitted as well!

That's why Romans 8:14 tells us about those *"...who are being led by the Spirit of God."* Know that when you face change, if you will be led by God's Spirit, you can be guaranteed that God is orchestrating **protection** on your behalf, regardless of the circumstances that may have brought about that change!

"But You, O Lord, are a shield around me."

(Psalm 3:3, NLT)

"If you pray only when you are in trouble, you are in trouble."

(Unknown)

Chapter Thirteen

The Power of Prayer

What a friend we have in Jesus
All our sins and griefs to bear!
What a privilege to carry,
Everything to God in prayer!
Oh, what peace we often forfeit,
Oh, what needless pain we bear
All because we do not carry
Everything to God in prayer![1]

This is a chapter I probably need not write too much about, but there is much to be put across. I have started by writing the lyrics of the very popular traditional hymn called *What a Friend We Have in Jesus*. The profound and deep words were written in 1885 as a poem by Joseph M. Scriven.

Why have I included this song in this chapter, let alone in this book? Because the story behind the song is very relevant to the subject matter of this book: **CHANGE**!

Joseph Scriven wrote this poem following certain tragedies and situations he had faced and endured. Joseph was born in Ireland, and he had a privileged upbringing, including a good education. His promising start saw him graduate from university and become a teacher. He also fell in love, and the young couple made plans to marry. However, just one day before their wedding, Joseph's fiancé fell from her horse and into a river where she drowned.

Grief-stricken, Joseph left Ireland and started a new life in Canada. There, he met and fell in love with another young lady, and marriage plans were made. But his new fiancé became very ill, and within weeks, she sadly died. Around a decade later, Joseph penned the story of his life in a poem that would become a well-loved hymn.

> *"Your greatest test, is when you are to bless someone else while you are going through your own storms."*
>
> (Rafael Garcia)[2]

As we've already seen, change comes in many guises — relocation, redundancy, sickness, promotion, marriage, births and deaths, to mention but a few. In all of these situations, there is one thing that is ALWAYS present, and we do it very well: **we talk about it**.

The issue to consider, or rather the question to ponder is this: what will people really be talking about?

What is the nature and content of these conversations surrounding change? It is easy to praise God and to talk positively when the outcomes of the change(s) faced culminate to something good and positive. But what do we really say when the outcomes or consequences of change are seemingly not so positive?

> *"When life is tough, pray.*
> *When life is great, pray."*
>
> (Unknown)

We certainly can learn a lot from Joseph Scriven. I cannot even begin to fathom the depths of his sorrow and pain at the tragic loss of two women he deeply loved and was about to wed. What would your reactions have been under these circumstances?

Bitterness? Anger? Complaining? A shaken faith? Disillusionment?

John the Baptist's faith was shaken because of the change he encountered. When things were good, and as a free man, John was able to publicly declare of Jesus, *"'Behold, the Lamb of God who takes away the sin of the world! This is He on behalf of whom I said, 'After me comes a Man who has a higher rank than I, for He existed before me.'"* (John 1:29-30). Yet, after he was imprisoned (**there's the change!**), John sent his disciples to ask Jesus, *"Are you the Messiah we've been expecting, or should we keep looking for someone else?'"* (Matthew 11:3 NLT).

With the gift of hindsight, it's very easy to judge John as one who doubted in the midst of trials. However, let us be open and honest about this – it is true that difficult circumstances can bring the worst out of us. When things were tough, I had questions, fears and doubts, too!

I believe Scriven went through a process of deep reflection, and at the end of it, exhibited a tremendously amazing quality – he kept God as God in his life. Scriven's words depict and define the essence of a right relationship with God. How did he do that? He did it through demonstrating possibly the most important of all the **P**s I have mentioned so far. What came out of his mouth was **PRAYER!**

The common tendency when we are faced with change (especially when it is challenging) is to withdraw from the very thing that is life-sustaining and circumstance-changing: **prayer**. That is why our peace is lost, and it is why we bear needless pain. Prayer keeps us connected to God.

> *"Prayer is where the action is."*
>
> (John Wesley)[3]

It is important for me to encourage you with this because I have to be real! I have to be up-front and state that prayer was not (and is still sometimes not) always my default position. Christopher usually tries to figure things out, and like many people, he sometimes waits until a crisis comes before praying. This should not be! We need to be people who pray as instructed by the Word of God – to pray without ceasing, for this is God's will for us (see 1 Thessalonians 5:16-18).

We need to re-evaluate how we do things. We can sometimes find ourselves where we should not be, mainly because of this very inclination to go to God as a 'last resort'. At times, God (not that He does not know) is usually the one we speak to last, having exhausted all our energies babbling to people and seeking their opinions before realising they can only help us so far!

If there were ever times when I got into the Word and into prayer, it was at times of change. There is nothing I can think of that could have sustained, strengthened and carried me through as did prayer. Very early on in my Christian walk, the Lord spoke to me through a Bible verse, and I have prayed over that scripture many times, especially during times of change. By doing so, it increased my faith in God's promises. Often, when circumstances changed, I heard many different voices in my ears (one of those being my own, while some voices were from other people), but it was only through prayer that I could apply the filters of the Spirit and begin to hear the voice I needed to hear – God's voice.

> *"…prayer does not change God, but changes the one who offers it."*
>
> (Sören Kierkegaard)[4]

117

The Bible gives us very good guidance and wisdom regarding this matter. It says this in Philippians chapter 4 verses 6-7: *"Be anxious for nothing, but in **everything by prayer** and supplication with thanksgiving let your requests be made known to God. And the peace of God, which surpasses all comprehension, will guard your hearts and your minds in Christ Jesus."*

This is confirmation that most changes will usually carry with them (to some degree) some anxieties, and the only way to embrace those changes without the anxieties is through prayer. Whenever we face change, prayer offers us something that nothing else can. It is in the place of prayer that we have communion with God, the place from which He can instruct, direct, comfort and ground us in His love. It is in prayer that we consolidate our faith (or relationship) with God, our Father!

Christ's disciples had many flaws, and they had much to learn. However, they did one noteworthy thing. Would you know what it was? I'll tell you – they asked Christ to teach them how to pray (Luke 11:1). I would like to think that they had seen Jesus praying often enough to attribute His authority, power and success to His lifestyle of prayer.

> *"The value of persistent prayer is not that He will hear us but that we will finally hear Him."*
>
> (William McGill)[5]

"Peace is always beautiful."

(Walt Whitman)[1]

Chapter Fourteen

The Umpire of Peace and Patience

S ome of you may be wondering why I started this book by quoting Hebrews 12:1-2. It's because I have realised that change is not unique to me. Change is not copyrighted to Christopher Chikwanah! Even Jesus, my Lord, underwent a lot of change. I was able to embrace change because I realised that I had to look to Jesus, the author and finisher of my faith. That passage of scripture in Hebrews talks about *'the joy set before Him'.* Jesus knew of the horrible fate awaiting Him at the cross. Yet, He called it 'joy' because He knew what the outcome would be!

Like Him, for the joy that was set before me, I endured the challenges and hardships of change, knowing that the end result would be great. Today, I can stand in awe of God when I see the end results of the change processes I have been through. The applicable **P** is this … the journey and the end product of change (if it is embraced accordingly) is **PEACE**. I may not have all I want and need, but I am at peace.

I believe that is what Paul was talking about when he said: *"...for I have learned to be **content** in whatever circumstances I am. I know how to get along with humble means, and I also know how to live in prosperity; in any and every circumstance I have learned the secret of being filled and going hungry, both of having abundance and suffering need."* (Philippians 4:11-12).

First and foremost, peace is a state of mind and a state of being.

People always confuse peace with having a lot of money, success, status, living the 'high life' and so forth. I am not saying those things are not desirable! However, if these are the things that are considered to constitute peace, then why do millionaires with all their possessions and riches commit suicide, get divorced, become alcoholics or get hooked on drugs? Simple: a lack of peace!

> *"When we put our problems in God's hands,*
> *He puts His peace in our hearts."*
>
> (Unknown)

Some of the changes and situations that we encounter can feel like we are truly going through the valley of the shadow of death. Be encouraged – do not fear. God is with you; His rod and His staff will comfort you (read Psalm 23)! 'Do not fear' simply means to be at peace, to be in a state of rest. God is known as Jehovah Shalom, translated 'Jehovah is peace'. You will not find peace if your sole trust is in jehovah money or jehovah status. Note the deliberate use of the small j!

Another **P** that goes hand-in-hand with peace is **PATIENCE**. Patience cannot be separated from peace. Our patience is usually the thing that is tested during times of change. We fail when we lose our patience, which leads to a loss of peace. What is the connection between patience and peace? Joyce Meyer is quoted to say, *"…patience is not the ability to wait, but the ability to keep a good attitude while waiting."*[2] I believe that the good attitude she is referring to is peace.

> *"Peace: It does not mean to be in a place where there is no noise, trouble or hard work.*
>
> *It means to be in the midst of those things and still be calm in your heart."*
>
> (Unknown)

Most competitive sporting matches need an umpire, without which there is no fairness. The umpire is the one to enforce the rules and keep the peace because not everyone plays fair. And just like an umpire is needed in the earthly realm, so is one needed in the spiritual realm, especially when we face change.

Make no mistake – the devil does not play fair. And if we do not ground ourselves in the 'rule book' of the Word, we will not have the umpire of peace.

Subsequently, we will be robbed of our destiny. Just look at Adam and Eve! The devil caused them to lose their peace concerning the way God had made them, what He had given them and where He had positioned them.

Their lack of peace and contentment caused them to ignore or forget that they were already created in the image of God, which meant they did not need to eat the forbidden fruit to be like Him (Genesis 1:26-27).

Additionally, the absence of peace in their lives resulted in them ignoring or forgetting the consequence of disobeying God (Genesis 2:17). In that state, they made an irrational choice, the ripple effects of which affected not only them but also every single person since then.

*"And let the **peace** (soul harmony which comes) from Christ rule (**act as umpire continually**) in your hearts [deciding and settling with finality all questions that arise in your minds, in that peaceful state] to which as [members of Christ's] one body you were also called [to live]. And be thankful (appreciative), [giving praise to God always]."* (Colossians 3:15, AMPC).

> *"Ego says, "Once everything falls in place, I'll feel peace."*
>
> *Spirit says, "Find your peace, and then everything will fall into place.""*
>
> (Marianne Williamson)[3]

"I'm stronger because I had to be, I'm smarter because of my mistakes, happier because of the sadness I've known and now wiser because I learned."

(Unknown)

Epilogue

I hope that you have received something from some of the personal life experiences and insights I have shared about the change processes I have been through. I am truly humbled to have shared my thoughts and perceptions with you.

This short book is by no means the final authority on embracing change. I am positive there are many other works on the subject. I hope this work has, even in a small way, helped you reflect on the changes you have already experienced. Furthermore, I hope it has equipped you to face the new changes you will inevitably encounter.

Let the losses and the changes we have faced, endured and overcome be the very things that we use to strengthen, comfort and encourage one another, not from a place of strength, perfection or judgement, but from a place of compassion.

Let the scars we bear not be worn with shame, but let them be the sign that we have been through battles and come out victorious. This is what writing this book has been all about! I believe this is the message that Paul was conveying when he wrote this to the Corinthians:

"Blessed be the God and Father of our Lord Jesus Christ, the Father of mercies and God of all comfort, who comforts us in all our affliction so that we will be able to comfort those who are in any affliction with the comfort with which we ourselves are comforted by God." (2 Corinthians 1:3-4).

So, let me remind you and encourage you with these closing thoughts … whatever changes you have been through or are going through right now, remember this – promotion, peace and prosperity are guaranteed through the change process, if you:

1. Don't allow **PAIN** to paralyse or disable you.

2. Don't violate or compromise your **PRINCIPLES**; choose rather to always live in line with God's Word. Always strive to do the right thing.

3. Utilise your **POTENTIAL**. Knowing your potential always helps you start over again.

4. Know and understand your **PRIORITIES**. Keep the important things important.

5. Do not lose your **PASSION**. Loss of passion breeds stagnation. The warning though is this – maintain your passion, but do not to become fanatical.

6. Know your **PURPOSE**. A lack of purpose is what causes despondency and despair.

7. Don't yield to **PRESSURE**. The thing about pressure is that if you fail to handle it appropriately, it will, at worst, crush you and make you crumble. At second best, it will make you a lump of coal, good only for a short while. But, if handled well, it will turn you into a diamond – this is the best possible outcome.

8. Always see each situation as bearing **POSSIBILITIES**, especially when you are out of your comfort zone.

9. Understand and embrace where God has **POSITIONED** you, regardless of how you got there.

10. Realise the fact that God is *always* **PROTECTING** you through the journey of change.

11. Make **PRAYER** your default position. It will help you see things from God's perspective.

12. Don't lose your **PEACE**. Peace must always remain your umpire. Remain **PATIENT**.

Change will require us to renew our minds and adopt new ways of thinking that translate into new ways of doing things. Change is about bringing new wine into our lives; it represents new seasons. As such, 'the old wineskins' of our thinking needs to be renewed to accommodate this change (read Matthew 9:17).

When you have faced change, you will never be the same again. Change is a new experience, and we should always be excited about the prospect of something new. Even God's mercies are NEW every morning (Lamentation 3:22-23). Oliver Wendall Holmes said that *"Every now and then a man's mind is stretched by a new idea or sensation, and never shrinks back to its former dimensions."*[1]

References

Every attempt has been made to reproduce quoted material accurately and with the correct attribution.

Introduction

1. Papers of John F. Kennedy. President's Office Files. Speech Files. Address in the Assembly Hall at the Paulskirche, Frankfurt, 25 June 1963.
2. Capra, F. (1996) *The Web of Life: A New Scientific Understanding of Living Systems.* United States. Anchor Books. p.80.
3. Attributed to Jim Rohn.

Chapter One

1. Attributed to Niccolò Machiavelli.
2. Attributed to Peter Strople.
3. Attributed to Oliver Goldsmith.

Chapter Two

1. Drake (2012) *High School Graduation Speech* [online]. 18 October 2012, Vaughan Road Academy, Ontario. Available from: https://www.youtube.com/watch?v=QBi-owfqK2A [accessed October 2018].

2. Cole, E. L. (2001) *Maximized Manhood: A Guide to Family Survival* Revised Ed. New Kensington. Whitaker House. p.163.

3. 33 Miles (2010) *Worth the Wait.* Tennessee. INO Records.

4. Warren, R. (2018) *You start healing the moment you stop blaming.* [Twitter] 26 March. Available at: https://twitter.com/RickWarren/status/978520850352648193 [accessed October 2018].

5. Lee. B. (1998) *The Power of Principle: Influence with Honor.* New York. Fireside. p.46.

Chapter Three

1. Ayivor, I. (2014) *The Great Hand Book of Quotes.* Self-published. p.42.

2. Armstrong, L. and Jenkins, S. (2003) *Every Second Counts.* Great Britain. Yellow Jersey Press. p.4.

3. Attributed to Lailah Gifty Akita.

Chapter Four

1. Attributed to Walter Cronkite.

2. Maxwell, J. C. (1993) *Developing the Leader Within You*. Nashville, TN. Thomas Nelson. p.94.

3. Attributed to Malcolm X.

Chapter Five

1. Attributed to Charles M. Schulz.

2. Watson, F. (2017) *Book 3 – Life Changes* Kindle Ed. Self-published. p.6.

3. Brinkley, T. L. (2013) *A Disciple's Dilemma: Series Sermons for Spiritual Growth*. Self-published. p.9.

4. Attributed to Robert Foster Bennett.

5. Meyer, J. (2001) *A Leader in the Making – Essentials to Being a Leader After God's own Heart*. New York. Warner Books. p.23.

6. Attributed to Brian Tracy.

7. Attributed to Catherine Pulsifer.

8. Bolsinger, T. (2015) *Canoeing the Mountains: Christian Leadership in Uncharted Territory*. Illinois. InterVarsity Press. p.142.

9. Attributed to Leo F. Buscaglia.

Chapter Six

1. Cole, E. L. (2003) *The Power of Potential: Maximize God's Principles to Fulfill Your Dreams* 2nd Edition. Texas. Watercolor Books. p.23-24.

2. McChrystal, S., Collins, T., Silverman, D. and Fussell, C. (2015) *Team of Teams: New Rules of Engagement for a Complex World* Kindle Ed. London. Penguin Publishing. Loc.14.

3. Attributed to Scott Caan.

Chapter Seven

1. Collins, J. (2011) *Good to Great and the Social Sectors*: *A Monograph to Accompany 'Good to Great'* Kindle Ed. New York. HarperCollins. Loc. 241-243.

2. Bolsinger, T. (2015) *Canoeing the Mountains: Christian Leadership in Uncharted Territory*. Illinois. InterVarsity Press. p.142.

3. Attributed to Jon Bon Jovi.

4. Attributed to David Gerrold.

5. Jakes, T. D. (2017) *If you can't figure out your purpose, figure out your passion. For your passion will lead you right into your purpose.* [Twitter]. 18 January 2017. Available at: https://twitter.com/bishopjakes/status/821688845972414464?lang=en [accessed October 2018].

Chapter Eight

1. Leider, R. (2015) *The Power of Purpose: Find Meaning, Live Longer, Better*. Oakland, CA. Berrett-Koehler Publishers. p.viii.

2. Bolsinger, T. (2015) *Canoeing the Mountains.* Illinois. InterVarsity Press. p.106, citing Heifetz, R. A. and Linsky, M. (2002) *Leadership on the Line: Staying Alive Through the Dangers of Leading.* Boston. Harvard Business School Press. p.11.

3. Goff, B. (2015) *We won't be distracted by comparison if we're captivated with purpose.* [Twitter]. 29 December. Available at: https://twitter.com/ bobgoff/status/681858284815552513 [accessed October 2018].

4. Dostoyevsky, F., translated by David McDuff (2003) *The Brothers Karamazov.* London. Penguin Books. p.332.

   This book was originally published in 1880.

5. Nietzsche, F. (1889) *Twilight of the Idols.* Public Domain.

Chapter Nine

1. Sweets, L. (2009) 'The Hero in the Hold' *Bones.* Season 4, episode 13, FOX TV, 5 February.

2. Attributed to Henry Kissinger.

3. Jobs, S. (2005) *Stanford University Commencement Address.* Available at: https:// news.stanford.edu/2005/06/14/jobs-061505/ [accessed October 2018].

4. Steinke, P. L. (2014) *Congregational Leadership in Anxious Times: Being Calm and Courageous No Matter What* Kindle Ed. Lanham, MD. Rowman & Littlefield. Loc.60.

5. Attributed to Lao Tzu.

6. Attributed to Quinton Jackson.

Chapter Ten

1. Attributed to Thích Nhất Hanh.

2. Attributed to David Cooperrider.

3. Attributed Margaret Drabble.

4. Attributed to Deepak Chopra.

5. Sebastian, K. *10 Tips for Embracing Change.* Blog post. Available at: https://hopepreneurs.com/category/change/ [accessed May 2017].

6. Chopra, D. (2014) *Instead of thinking outside the box, get rid of the box.* [Twitter]. 19 February. Available at: https://twitter.com/DeepakChopra/status/436274254129029121 [accessed October 2018].

Chapter Eleven

1. Attributed to Mason Cooley.

Chapter Thirteen

1. Scriven, J. M. (1855) *What a Friend We Have in Jesus.* Public Domain. Available at: https://us.search.ccli.com/songs/1782773/what-a-friend-we-have-in-jesus [accessed October 2018].

2. Attributed to Rafael Garcia.

3. Attributed to John Wesley.

4. Kierkegaard, S. (2009) *Purity of Heart is to Will One Thing*. USA. Feather Trail Press. p.25. *This book was originally written in 1846.*

5. Attributed to William McGill.

Chapter Fourteen

1. Whitman, W. (2015) *Leaves of Grass*. Great Britain. William Collins. p.92. *The quote comes from Whitman's poem, 'The Sleepers', which was included in his first edition of 'Leaves of Grass' in 1855.*

2. Meyer, J. (1995) *Battlefield of the Mind: Winning the Battle in Your Mind*. New York. Warner Books. p.223.

3. Williamson, M. (2013) *Ego says, "Once everything falls in place, I'll feel peace." Spirit says, "Find your peace, and then everything will fall into place."* [Twitter]. 10 August. Available at: https://twitter.com/marwilliamson/status/366263645572829185 [accessed October 2018].

Epilogue

1. Holmes, O. W. (1858) *The Autocrat of the Breakfast-Table* ebook. Public Domain. Loc. 3279 & 3286.

Lightning Source UK Ltd.
Milton Keynes UK
UKHW021845250421
382604UK00002B/2

9 781838 186104